Shigeru Miyamoto

Influential Video Game Designers

Series Editors:

Carly A. Kocurek
Jennifer deWinter

Shigeru Miyamoto

Super Mario Bros., Donkey Kong, The Legend of Zelda

Jennifer deWinter

Bloomsbury Academic
An imprint of Bloomsbury Publishing Inc

B L O O M S B U R Y
NEW YORK · LONDON · NEW DELHI · SYDNEY

Bloomsbury Academic

An imprint of Bloomsbury Publishing Inc

1385 Broadway	50 Bedford Square
New York	London
NY 10018	WC1B 3DP
USA	UK

www.bloomsbury.com

**BLOOMSBURY and the Diana logo are trademarks
of Bloomsbury Publishing Plc**

First published 2015

Library of Congress Cataloging-in-Publication Data
DeWinter, Jennifer.
Shigeru Miyamoto: Super Mario Bros., Donkey Kong, the Legend of
Zelda/Jennifer DeWinter.
pages cm
Summary: "An in-depth creative and cultural analysis of Shigeru Miyamoto,
the 'father of modern video gaming'"– Provided by publisher.
Includes bibliographical references and index.
ISBN 978-1-62892-468-8 (hardback) – ISBN 978-1-62892-388-9 (paperback)
1. Miyamoto, Shigeru, 1952- 2. Video games–Design–History. 3. Video games
industry–History. 4. Computer programmers–Japan–Biography. I. Title.
GV1469.3.D49 2015
794.8–dc23
2015000344

ISBN: HB: 978-1-6289-2468-8
PB: 978-1-6289-2388-9
ePub: 978-1-6289-2387-2
ePDF: 978-1-6289-2386-5

Series: Influential Video Game Designers

Typeset by Deanta Global Publishing Services, Chennai, India
Printed and bound in the United States of America

Contents

List of Figures

Acknowledgments

This book is a long time in coming. It started from an idea hatched in the Game Studies SIG at the Southwest Popular and American Culture Association (SW PACA) conference. A number of us in attendance were ruminating about a lack of game studies scholarship that attended to game designers. We were seeing presentations on close readings of games, game theories, and game creation, but nothing on the people behind the texts that we were considering. Strange, considering that literature attends to authors, film attends to directors, and art attends to artists. About the same time, I was teaching a game design class, and all of the books were about lenses, rules, challenges, and puzzles. There were no books that I could assign students that gave them insight into a game designer's vision or process.

With this context in mind, I have a lot of people to acknowledge. First and foremost, Carly Kocurek, my coeditor of this series—you saw promise and need and were willing to do the hard work with me. Judd Ruggill, thank you for convening the Game Studies group every year at SW PACA. And to my fellow game scholars who converge there every year (in alphabetical order): Suellen Adams, Marlin Bates, Stefan Boehme, Joseph Chaney, Andrew Chen, Tobias Conradi, Steven Conway, Michael De Anda, James Fleury, Greg Gillespie, Harrison Gish, Daniel Griffin, Kati Heljakka, Damien Huffer, Ryan Kaufman, Owen Leach, Ken McAllister, Kevin Moberly, Ryan Moeller, Devin Monnens, Aki Nakamura, Randy Nichols, Rolf Nohr, David O'Grady, Steven Ortega, Francisco Ortega-Grimaldo, Marc Ouellette, Matthew Thomas Payne, Martin Riggenbach, Theo Rohle, Tom Rose, Ron Scott, Jason Thompson, Samuel Tobin, Stephanie Vie, William White, Clayton Whittle, Serjoscha Wiemer, Megan Winget, Josh Zimmerman, and everyone else who has dropped in and out over the years.

Also, at my institution, I would like to thank my colleagues in Humanities and Arts (HUA) and in the Interactive Media and Game

Development (IMGD) program. In HUA, a special thanks to Constance Clark, Jennifer Rudolph, and Kris Boudreau for their support and friendship throughout this process. In IMGD, I would like to especially thank Mark Claypool for his many years as director and now Rob Lindemann, our new director. In addition, Dean O'Donnell and Ralph Sutter—thanks for beers and brainstorming! And thank you too to Joe Farbrook, David Finkel, Brian Moriary, George Phillies, Chuck Rich, Josh Rosenstock, Britt Snyder, and Keith Zizza.

In writing this book, I also traveled to Rochester, New York, to use the excellent resources at The Strong National Museum of Play. So a special thanks to Shannon Simons for fielding all of my requests for Japanese materials, and to Jon-Paul C. Dyson, Beth Lathrop, and Tara Winner for their research help during my hours at your archive. Also, Jim Bowman and Meg Gillio, thank you for many music-filled Rochester evenings when all you wanted to do was stop talking about video games.

Early in this process, the book series received external reviews, and those comments helped to shape this book. So to Mark J. P. Wolf, Henry Lowood, and Steven Conway, thank you for your guidance. Also, thank you to the anonymous reviewer of this book—your comments helped to shape it into what it now is. And thank you, Angelia Giannone, for your excellent indexing work.

Now this actual book would not exist without two people: First, Nick DeMarinis, research assistant extraordinaire! Thank you for reading more Iwata Asks interviews with me than anyone else in the world. And Aaron McGaffey for support and excellent photographic help. You are long suffering, and I still appreciate that.

Finally, what would be the fun of writing an acknowledgments section if I didn't acknowledge my children, constant distractions that they are. Rowan McGaffey and Freya deWinter, thank you for playing *Super Mario Galaxy* with me.

Foreword

Carly A. Kocurek and Jennifer deWinter

During the initial rise of video gaming, most players would have been hard-pressed to name a game designer. While company founders like Nolan Bushnell and H. R. "Pete" Kaufmann made the news with some regularity, the design of games was treated as a technical practice, and titles by and large went uncredited, their designers anonymous and unknown. These same designers were often jacks-of-all-trades, responsible not only for the game's design, but also for its writing, artwork, music, and sound. Will* Robinett's act of defiance, the planting of his own name inside Atari's *Adventure*, was an impulsive protest of the anonymity. After all, Robinett's effort to cram the complicated game into the cartridge's limited memory space was an act of technological wizardry for which he, like his colleagues, would receive little to no formal recognition or reward. Robinett's hidden signature became the first Easter egg in video game history, and Robinett has gone down in the annals of game history as a skilled designer.

In the years between Robinett's subversive effort to include his John Hancock in *Adventure* and the present, the role of the game designer has become increasingly visible. Designers are interviewed in magazines and they sit on panels at conferences. They are recognized and increasingly organized. The International Game Developers Association now boasts over 12,000 members worldwide. Game design programs abound at universities across the United States and across the globe; there are so many that the *Princeton Review*, long-standing quantifier of higher education program quality, now offers rankings of game design programs at both the undergraduate and graduate level. The professionalization of the game industry has brought with it a growing awareness and visibility of game designers.

✱ typo: Warren

In launching this series on influential game designers, we aim to contribute to the study of and discourse surrounding game design by focusing on human agents. This series derived from a simple question: What would it mean to consider game designers the way we frequently consider film directors? So often, discourse around game design has to do with design components: how to integrate puzzles, how to write a game story, how to design a level. This approach, of course, has value, situated as it is in teaching the basic mechanics of game creation. However, designers concern themselves not with the component parts but with the whole experience, translating those experiences into systems. The act of play turns systems back into experiences, there for players to share with the game designer's vision. Influential game designers create new systems, new experiences, shaping future games and the experiences of players.

This is not a charge into the churning debate of whether or not games are art; rather, it is an invitation to consider the creative labor of game design on its own merits. Game design is an act of creation, of building, of communication, of cultural production, and, of course, of design. That process of creation is worthy of study in its own right. The impact of games is well documented. Specific games such as *World of Warcraft* or *BioShock* or specific genres such as first-person shooters or RPGs receive careful consideration. The impact of game designers—of the people who engineer the stories and experiences that drive those same games—should be equally obvious; yet it remains understudied. Creative vision remains fairly invisible. The problem with this is that agency also becomes invisible. Contemporary discussions tend to focus on games as agents, teaching sexism or violence through nefarious channels to an always-susceptible audience. Or it focuses on players, agents in their own actions and interactions with games and possibly to other players. The absence of the designer may have to do with an extension of Barthes' 1967 "Death of the Author" argument. In this, Barthes argues that we cannot know author intentionality and that meaning cannot be parsed through biographical data. Rather, every reading of a text always happens here and now, interpreted through the very specific context of consumption. And this has great resonance with game studies, which emphasizes the agency of the player in cocreating a game through play. No game is the same because no play session is the same. We do not disagree with this, yet we cannot ignore that many of these game designers, these authors, are in fact not dead. They had intentions, visions, and experiences that they encoded into the game, and they negotiated those with the player through the medium of television, arcade, and computer.

We have chosen to launch this series with a book on one of the best known of game designers, Shigeru Miyamoto, the mastermind behind such iconic and long-standing game franchises as Donkey Kong, Mario Bros., and Zelda. We argue here that even when we are talking about complicated systems of production and distribution, it's imperative to think about how human agency plays out. Thus, as we develop the historiography of games, we provide a focus on design through the lens of the designer. Miyamoto, then, is a particular provocative subject because of his involvement in both the design of game software and game hardware. Further, his career, dating from the 1970s, spans much of the history of video games. His influence can be seen throughout the game industry—he has created and defined a number of game genres—and throughout popular cultures at large. Miyamoto's games and systems show up in other forms in movies, television, magazines, books, orchestras, schools, dance clubs, rap music, and children's lunch boxes. And as Chapter 1 indicates in the title, Miyamoto makes perfect sense for the inaugural book of the Influential Game Designers book series: He is the father of modern video games.

The Father of Modern Video Games

Shigeru Miyamoto is a Japanese game designer who entered the game development industry serendipitously, joining Nintendo in 1977 after his father lined up a general design job for him. The first game design challenge he faced was *Donkey Kong* (Nintendo 1981), a resounding success and the first of many successful franchises, including Mario, Zelda, Nintendogs, Starfox, and Pikmin, among others. It was this initial success, however, that propelled him into a career as a game designer, producer, director, and hardware developer, influencing the industry throughout his now forty years at Nintendo. Unlike many influential game designers, his story as a designer has been closely linked to the success of Nintendo, and it is a symbiotic relationship that has mutually benefited both. Indeed, books that analyze the history and role of Nintendo, such as Jeff Ryan's *Super Mario: How Nintendo Conquered America* (2011) and Chris Kohler's *Power Up: How Japanese Video Games Gave the World an Extra Life* (2004), do so by treating Nintendo and Shigeru Miyamoto synonymously.

Miyamoto's games are often among the top-selling games for Nintendo consoles (see numbers in the Gameography of this book). Further, the importance of his games has even been recognized by the 2009 *Guinness Book of World Records*, which named *Super Mario Kart* (Nintendo 1992) as the most influential game of all time (Ivan 1999).

Shigeru Miyamoto has discussed a number of design elements that guide his work:

- The strong connection to childhood and joy;
- The influences of nature and the natural world; and

- A desire to share a common feeling—*kyokan*—so that designers can feel closeness with players and players can be immersed in the experience of the game.

He is also credited with particular attention to narrative detail and artistic expression, both in visual design and music/sound design. In addition to these much-discussed design philosophies, hardware development serves a key role in Miyamoto's corpus of work. Miyamoto learned hardware during his early collaboration with Gunpei Yokoi, an engineer and designer at Nintendo. Further, Nintendo is a rare company in that it focuses on both hardware and software development, so Miyamoto has had opportunities to design the whole game system. Indeed, Miyamoto has been at the helm of a number of hardware designs, culminating in his work on the Wii and subsequently the Wii U. Further, the sheer number of patents filed by Miyamoto evidences his design work influencing more than the structure of the games that he releases.

Shigeru Miyamoto's design vision can best be described as "fun entertainment." This, according to Miyamoto, articulates well onto Nintendo's corporate strategy; his personal vision of game design resonates with his company. In his 2007 GDC Keynote entitled "A Creative Vision," Miyamoto explained: "My initial focus and my primary focus throughout development is not these individual elements of the game. When I am creating a game, what I always try to envision, what I always think about, is the core element of fun within the game. And to do that, I imagine one thing, and that's the face of the player when he or she is experiencing the game, not any individual part of the game." To emphasize his point, Miyamoto showed slides of people of all ages crowded around consoles and handheld devices, smiling and exclaiming their delight. Making people cry or feel scared, according to a Miyamoto interview in the documentary *The Video Game Revolution* (Palmer 2004), is easy; however, he explained, "making them laugh, feel excitement and pleasure is difficult." And, if he achieves his goals, then he will have created video games for a broad market, something that everyone will play.

More than his design vision, market saturation is Miyamoto's goal in the same way that it is Nintendo's goal: Games are big business. In a glib way, he acknowledged this at his 1999 GDC keynote, concluding with this remark: "My friends, let us design unique, fun software with new appeal. Let us take on new challenges so that the world of gaming is not left behind as a separate, closed off world. And in the process, let's see if we can't make a little money" ("Conference Keynote"). Miyamoto was more to the point, however, during his Digital Content Expo 2009 speech in Japan, when he explained, "We are making products, not works of art"; further Miyamoto instructs all of the Nintendo employees to refer to games similarly as products (qtd in Ikeya 2009, my translation). This business focus is important when attending to Miyamoto as a game designer because, according to him, he designs games for broad reach, specifically targeting women, children, and housewives in addition to a more traditional construct of male players in a way that other key designers often do not. Yet his entrance into the game industry was, at best, accidental.

The birth of a game auteur

This origin story has firmly passed into video game legend: In 1977, Hiroshi Yamauchi, the president of Nintendo, hired Shigeru Miyamoto and assigned him to the planning department. This part of the story sounds fairly mundane. It is rather the context that makes this particular hire the stuff of myths and legends.

Born in 1952, Miyamoto grew up in Sonobe, Kyoto, a rural town in the Kansai region. He loved reading and drawing manga (Japanese comics), listening to music, doing puppet shows, and wandering the countryside. While wandering, he came across a cave, which features prominently in his own recounting of his formative life moments. According to Miyamoto, he would often return to the cave to watch platonic shadows dance across the wall, and after he mustered the courage, he brought a lantern to explore the darkness. It was these early explorations into the unknown natural world that would provide the inspiration for *The Legend of Zelda* (Nintendo 1986). Further, these early wanderings would offer the experiential blueprint for the ways in which a Japanese sensibility of nature would influence his work.

Following his childhood, Miyamoto entered Kanazawa Bijutsu Kōgei Daigaku, or Kanazawa Art and Industrial Design University, to study Industrial Design and Engineering. By his own admission, he was a terrible student, taking five years to finish his four-year degree because he rarely attended classes and focused instead on playing banjo for his college band. I do not want to brush past the training that Miyamoto had in industrial engineering as so often happens in this origin story. As such, I will return to an examination of the discipline of industrial engineering and design later in this chapter. However, it is important to note here that Miyamoto studied in a field that emphasized human interactions in complex processes or systems through analysis and design, and this training came to bear on his design process after he joined Nintendo. Upon graduation, Miyamoto didn't have a job lined up and thought that he might try his hand as a manga artist. His father, in response to this development, arranged an interview with Hiroshi Yamauchi, the president of Nintendo at the time. Miyamoto showcased some of his industrial design projects, such as a three-way seesaw, children's clothes hangers with animals on them, and a clock designed for an amusement park. Miyamoto was hired and given a job in the planning department as an artist.[1]

The exigency for Miyamoto to become a game designer came with Minoru Arakawa's attempt to break into the US market. Arakawa was the head of the American branch of Nintendo at the time, and the Nintendo home office sent him 3,000 units of the arcade *Radar Scope* (Nintendo 1979) to sell in North America. However, there was a lag between the time that the game was released in Japan and when it was made available in the United States, so the hype had died down, and the game did not perform well in the United States. Arakawa was able to sell only 1,000 units, leaving 2,000 in a New Jersey

---

[1] Miyamoto's success is largely based on good timing. Nintendo was not a video game giant at the time, and the leadership was willing to take more chances. Indeed, in an interview, Miyamoto said: "I often say to Mr Iwata: 'If I was applying for a job here today, I, with my actual college degree, would probably not have been employed by Nintendo!'" (qtd in Totu 2009).

warehouse. Arakawa convinced Nintendo's president Yamauchi to develop a new game for the *Radar Scope* hardware in order to move the remaining cabinets, and Yamauchi agreed. However, according to Ryan in his book *Super Mario: How Nintendo Conquered America* (2011), Yamauchi hedged his bets: "Yamauchi's top designers were all busy on their own games, and he wasn't going to pull any of them off their projects for this rush job. So he announced an internal competition for conversion ideas. He received several ideas from a surprising source, a boyish, shaggy-haired staff artist with an industrial design degree but no previous game experience" (21). Enter Shigeru Miyamoto.

Yamauchi paired Miyamoto up with Gunpei Yokoi, a game designer and the hardware designer behind the Game & Watch game systems and later the Game Boy (a relationship that I explain in more detail later in this chapter). Important for this story is Yokoi's design philosophy of *Kareta Gijutsu no Shuhei Shikou*, or "lateral thinking of withered technology" (Donovan 2010, 205), which focused on repurposing existing yet dated technologies for new developments. Yokoi used existing technologies, such as monochromatic LCD screens, for his subsequent development of Game Boy, to keep the device light and help conserve battery life, which also helped to keep the price down. Further, Yokoi applied his years of designing for the Game & Watch series and successfully made the argument that the Game Boy should be a cartridge-based system, ensuring longer monetizing possibilities for Nintendo's profitability. This method shaped how Miyamoto would approach hardware and software development throughout his career.

Lateral thinking of withered technology articulated well onto the repurposing of the old *Radar Scope* cabinets. The cabinet already had fixed affordances in hardware. Miyamoto was tasked with a design process challenge, and in responding to this challenge, he brought to bear his aesthetic talents with his industrial engineering training. Miyamoto explained during an "Iwata Asks" interview that he would play video games constantly, and people would often crowd around him as he played. He said: "As I was originally an industrial designer, I would analyze those games while I played them, trying to figure out what it was about the way the games were put together that made them enjoyable and made people want to play them again" ("Mario Couldn't Jump at First" n.d.). Indeed, the first arcade game that Miyamoto was drawn to was Space Invaders, which was such a success in Japan that the nation had to quadruple the production of 100-yen coins (Kohler, 19).[2] While analyzing the games, Miyamoto tried to determine why players continued to pay more money to extend play, and he determined that the players were doing so because they were mad at themselves. He discussed these theories with Yokoi, and he translated his understanding of this and accounted for it in the design process ("Mario Couldn't Jump at First" n.d.).

Story-wise, *Donkey Kong* started as an iteration of a previous intellectual property: Popeye. Miyamoto's original design had Popeye eating spinach and climbing platforms to get to Brutus at the top. However, for undisclosed reasons, Nintendo was unable to develop the Popeye game at that time, so Miyamoto had to invent new characters, which saw the birth of Mario, the now iconic character for the Nintendo universe. So instead of the Popeye story, Miyamoto imagined a different love triangle between a stubborn ape (hence "Donkey Kong"), a "Lady," and "Jumpman." Miyamoto designed Jumpman in the *mukokuseki* manga aesthetic, or that of the ethnically generic character. This proved an excellent design choice for an internationally distributed game. And finally, in *Donkey Kong*, the character's name was Jumpman because of his ability to jump. This seems tautological; however, this was the first game to require jumping to traverse gaps and spring over enemies, and this development provided the core game mechanic of the platformer game (GamesRadar 2010).

Miyamoto was not just iterating on characters—Popeye to Jumpman—he was iterating on hardware as well. Miyamoto originally

---

[2] Japanese arcade games are based on a 100-yen standard, which has approximately the same buying power as a US dollar. This standard is credited with allowing Japan to avoid the video game crash of 1983 (Crecente 2011).

conceived of *Donkey Kong* as a side-scrolling game. However, the hardware that was available in the Rader Scope cabinets would not support side scrolling. This material limitation required some rethinking of the original design so that the eventual *Donkey Kong* would be comprised of four screens that represented different 25-meter levels of a steel structural building, making the total building 100 meters tall. Ultimately, Miyamoto wanted the game to progress as a chase, which required multiple levels. In telling this development story, Ryan reports that the "development team was baffled; variations on a theme were what sequels were for" (27). Add to this Miyamoto's desire for an introductory animation—Donkey Kong carrying Lady to the top and then damaging the environment to stop Jumpman—and the development scope of this game expanded in demand and skill. And as a final touch, Donkey Kong had a soundtrack that was not the normal beeps and explosions of arcade games. And while there is some confusion concerning who is responsible for the music—Sheff claims that it was Miyamoto in his book *Game Over* (1994), and Nintendo credits Yukio Kaneoka ("Yukio Kaneoka" 2011)—the fact is that this game had cinematic attention with a storyline, cut scenes, and a soundtrack. A first in game history.

Miyamoto did not limit his design choices to the narrative motivation of the game. He designed Jumpman as a character with visual idiosyncrasies, a career as a plumber (the overalls were the visual cue for this), and a superhuman ability to defy gravity with every jump. Jumpman got his name, Mario, only when Arakawa became annoyed with a warehouse owner in Seattle from whom Nintendo rented space. This landlord named Mario purportedly threatened eviction and threw a jump-up-and-down fit.

On July 9, 1981, *Donkey Kong* was released. All 2,000 converted arcade units were sold. One year later, Nintendo had sold 60,000 *Donkey Kong* machines and had earned $180 million (Kent 2001). Mario would go on to become one of the most iconic characters of the twentieth century.

The dialectics of design: Miyamoto's influences and products

While people often recognize the influence that Miyamoto has had on the game industry and in their personal histories playing games, the fact is that writing about Miyamoto as a game auteur presents a number of challenges. These challenges arise mainly because he is involved in game design, hardware development, and software development and patenting. Further, it needs to be explicitly stated that Miyamoto, as a Japanese citizen, comes from a fundamentally different culture than Western audiences, so what seem to be personal idiosyncrasies or brilliant innovations make a type of historical sense when viewed in cultural context. To try and account for his historical and cultural context as well as attend to the objects that he created and what those objects tell us about design, I have created four categories through which one can understand Miyamoto's work (see also Figure 1.1): (1) his cultural

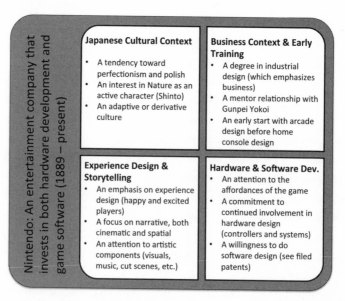

Figure 1.1 Shigeru Miyamoto design matrix.

and historical context; (2) his formal training in the business of design and games; (3) his focus on hardware and software development; and (4) his approach to experience design and storytelling. These categories are shown as quadrants in Figure 1.1 and are depicted as being bound up inextricably in a history with Nintendo, a toy company that focuses on entertainment business opportunities.

In the following sections, I will briefly sketch Miyamoto's design process and vision, fleshing out the claims suggested in Figure 1.1. Before doing so, however, it is worth noting that these categories are not isolated. For example, Miyamoto's mentor relationship with Yokoi directly informs his commitment to hardware. Also, hardware limitations have shaped Miyamoto's designs. Even the ways in which he structures narratives and characters have a lot to do with his cultural context. Thus, what this structure provides is a way to talk about each of these categories as part of Miyamoto's auteurship as well as speak to the ways that each of these categories change and influence the next. There are limitations to this method, however. I must simplify what might otherwise be complex processes or design visions in order to speak to component parts. Or, conversely, I may seem to go on tangents in discussing narratives when readers really just want to understand the story design and the influence of Zelda, for example.

Before considering each of these categories, I would like to first turn my attention briefly to a quick history of Nintendo, its early practices in the video game market, and its continued investment in hardware and games because it is in this context that Miyamoto works. Indeed, in creating Figure 1.1, Nintendo as business context encompasses Miyamoto as designer, so much so that we should not consider it a separate category but rather the foundation from which Miyamoto was trained and continues to work.

Nintendo: Developing in a closed market

Nintendo, like other game companies in Japan, started to look to games as a viable entertainment opportunity because of a confluence of events: *PONG* (Atari 1972) was released and was commercially viable; the Japanese population had more discretionary income due to the construction boom of the 1960s; and Japanese citizens started to demand and were awarded more free time (previously, it was common for Japanese "salary men" to work seven days a week). During this time, Taito and Sega were developing games for the Japanese market, and Namco focused its attention on importing Atari games (Pettus 2012; Kohler 2004). Nintendo saw an opportunity to simultaneously develop hardware and software, first for the arcade market, but early on the company set its sights on developing games that were portable and cheap to manufacture. Nintendo, like its competitors, already had close ties to older entertainment and gambling media. Nintendo, which literally means "place where luck is in the hands of heaven," started as Yamauchi Nintendo Playing Cards, the Kyoto-based *hanafuda* playing card manufacturer. While its work in playing cards—both Japanese *hanafuda* and Western-style decks called *toranpu* (trump)—was lucrative for the company because of yakuza-based high-stakes gambling, Hiroshi Yamauchi saw an opportunity to expand into computer games by becoming the distributor of the Magnavox Odyssey game system in Japan in 1974. Later, in response to the commercial success of *Space Invaders* (Taito 1978), Gunpei Yokoi of Nintendo created the Game & Watch series, the first entry of which combined a digital clock with the computer game *Ball*, in 1980 (see Figure 1.2).

The success of the Game & Watch series led to 30 million units being sold during the series' first eleven years (Donovan, 155). While computer technology allowed for the commercial success of games, the important role of the game designer was about to emerge in the early 1980s, and the dual emphasis on story and technology would spur computer games to become a more immersive medium. And no designer's name is more important in this early era than that of Shigeru Miyamoto. However, before attending further to Miyamoto's origin story, I would like to first consider the protectionist policies that Nintendo used to corner the home video game market because this is the context that enabled Miyamoto to learn and thrive in his art.

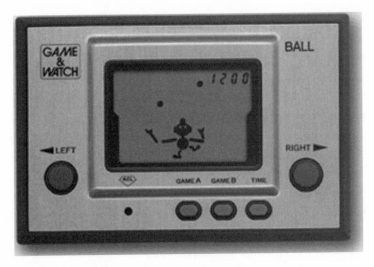

Figure 1.2 Game & Watch *Ball* (Nintendo 1980).
(Image retrieved from Wikipedia)

In the early 1980s, Yamauchi was poised to replicate Atari's success in the home console market. He ordered the development of the Nintendo Famicom (short for "family computer"), asking designer Masayuki Uemura to "create a console that was not only a year ahead of the competition in technology but also a third of the price of the Epoch Cassette Vision" (Donovan, 158). The Nintendo Famicom was released in July of 1983 and by the end of the year had sold over a million units. Due to the pressures of the company's success, Yamauchi created a new licensing agreement for other game publishers—an agreement that still dominates the computer game market to this day. In essence, publishers had to pay cash upfront to create a game, and then share a cut of the profits with Nintendo. Also, Nintendo could veto the release of any game, ensuring quality and content control. As a result, violent and sex-based games were banned from the console, and violent games were licensed only after the ESRB rating system was enacted, thus ensuring Nintendo's commitment to the "family computer" of entertainment.

While the reasons for its success are multifaceted, Izushi and Aoyama attribute Nintendo's ability to displace earlier competing products from Tommy and Bandai (both Japanese companies) to "price competitiveness, its ability to deliver original mega-hit software such as *Super Mario Brothers* (1985), and its initial alliances with best-selling arcade video games" (2006, 1847): in other words, a dual focus on hardware and software, an eye to an eager consumer market, and policies that ensured that they controlled approximately 90 percent of the home console market through the use of exclusivity agreements. In discussing these exclusivity agreements and the effects that they had on the burgeoning Sega company, Pettus writes, "When you own 90% of the world's largest videogame market, then you don't have to play fair. That only leaves 10% for your competition, which in theory means they never should be able to catch up with you no matter what they put out" (26). And while the market to develop games for consoles opened up in the 1990s, in no small part due to Trip Hawkins' strong-arm techniques against Sega in the early days of EA, Nintendo continued and continues to release exclusive games developed for their consoles, often developed in-house.

This leads to a sad tale concerning Sega's rise and fall (a tale that is then parodied in the manga and subsequent anime *Aoi Sekai no Chuushin de* (Yanagisawa 2007), which chronicles the war between the Segua Kingdom and the Ninterudo Empire in the land of Consume). More germane to this book, however, is that this lopsided market share coupled with the emergence of exclusive development agreements is the corporate and historical framework that launched Shigeru Miyamoto. Miyamoto entered game design early in its modern history at a time when Nintendo was developing hardware and software in tandem. The company offered the hardware at a reduced cost by using older or cheaper technologies (an approach to hardware design resonates with Gompei Yokoi's philosophy, which I discuss later in this chapter). Further, Nintendo was early in the home console market, and they established their brand as a family-friendly entertainment company. This historical context coupled with exclusivity agreements ensured that Miyamoto was designing in a protected space for a console that had significant market saturation (61.91 million units sold of this 1983 home console [VGChartz, "Platform Totals" 2014], a number that would not be surpassed until a decade later with Sony's foray into the market with the PlayStation [1994]). To present this context is not to diminish Miyamoto's design vision or influence, but this history did ensure that Miyamoto's work was highlighted and appreciated by more people early in video game development. So while he wasn't "there first," he was still early enough that a lot of what he contributed—narrative, multiple integrated levels, superior sound tracks, and even jumping characters—were firsts in game history.

A Japanese cultural context

Reams of paper can be expended on explaining the Japanese cultural context in general and how Nintendo and Miyamoto are both products of that culture. This is a culture that uses the idea of "play" or *asobi* (遊び) for both children and adults: "The children are playing outside" (*sotode kodomotachi ga asondeimasu*) or "I'm going to go hang out (play) with my friends" (*tomodachito asobini ikimasu*). Play is opposed to serious work, a topic that Huizinga (1955) explores in his seminal book *Homo Ludens*. Linguistically, though, play is not relegated to children's space. The nonserious work of adults, too, is described as play. So while in the United States, play among adults tends to be used only when speaking of sports, Japanese people will use play for a range of activities that English linguistically sidesteps with "go see," "hang out," or "go have fun." Thus, when Miyamoto is talking about creating games that everyone can play, games that bring joy to children and adults, he is not necessarily talking about making childhood joy available to adults. He is simply creating video games that allow for play in new spaces for any generation of user.

Another major design thread is Miyamoto's self-professed love of nature. Throughout his career, he has often told tales of his childhood, of going out into the woods and exploring caves. But in adding

Japanese context here, we see this childhood nostalgia linked to a version of nature that is active and spiritual and has its expression in Japanese Shintoism. Shinto is a Japanese natural religion (as opposed to revealed or organized religion; see Ama 2005) in that it is formed rather organically as mores and integrated gradually into the lives of communities. The underlying tenet belongs to folklore, providing both origin myths and a way to understand the natural world as sentient, full of *kami*, or spirits, who belong to nature (Ono and Woodard 1962). Kami can be the spirits of trees, of mountains, or even of important or great people. These kami can be benevolent or antagonistic, but they are manifestations of desire and essence and can be called upon to intercede for a person. This influence is most strongly seen in Zelda, which has spirit characters such as the fairy Navi; natural objects that are sentient such as the Deku Tree; a natural environment that acts as a character, often with maps changing color to mimic internal lives; and a mystery of the unknown. Indeed, the Great Deku Tree is the guardian of the forest, which the Deku Tree explains in *The Legend of Zelda: Ocarina of Time* (1998). In announcing himself in this way, the tree echoes the very definition of Shinto kami: "kami are the guardian spirits of the land, occupations, and skills" (Ono and Woodard, 7). Thus, Miyamoto's design becomes an extension of his own cultural narratives.

From these basic design elements, the other categories that I would like to discuss in developing the framework of this book attend mostly to development processes. In addition to basing his sense of play and fun in a Japanese context, we can see evidence throughout his works that Miyamoto subscribes to derivative innovation; that is, he takes ideas that have already been developed, both his own and others, and uses those to start the next development cycle, often making those ideas better. This mode of innovation is functionally well documented in Japan, from the early importation of Dutch medicine during the Tokugawa era that was heralded as "Western Medicine, Japanese Essence" to Kentucky Fried Chicken as a unique Japanese food commodity today (see, for example, Tobin's *Re-Made in Japan: Everyday Life and Consumer Taste in a Changing Society* [1992] or Alverez and

Kolker's documentary *The Japanese Version* [1991]). While these are cultural examples, this tradition is also visible in the Japanese business culture, leading people to claim that Japanese innovation is stunted by the fact that they just adapt other people's ideas. In contemporary news, this idea is probably best expressed by Michael Fitzpatrick's 2013 BBC article "Can Japan Reboot Its Anti-Innovation Start-Up Culture?" Yet this harsh view ignores the ways in which adaptation leads to new innovation through incremental change. As Shenkar (2010) argues in "Copycats: How Smart Companies Use Imitation to Gain a Strategic Edge," imitation can generate huge profits by saving on R&D costs, marketing, and advertising investments that are typically made in the first iteration. But this imitation and innovation must fit into a Japanese cultural context, for as Herbig and Jacobs (1997) explain, "The Japanese made a deliberate decision 100 years ago to concentrate their resources on social innovations and to imitate, import, and adapt technical innovations (Drucker 1985), to utilize Western technology but not at the expense of their own culture" (761). A new idiom suggests itself: Adapted Western Ideas, Japanese Essence.

This Japanese approach to innovation complements media innovation well, which tends to adhere to the cinematic idiom "tried and true with a twist." Games designers rely on players' motivations to learn game mechanics and then expect a certain amount of transferability of those skills from one game to another. Throughout this book, I will speak to examples of this complementary nature, but to illustrate my point here, I would like to discuss the character Mario, who first appeared on computer screens in *Donkey Kong*. Miyamoto had very real pixel limitations, but I will ignore that for now. Miyamoto originally wanted to be a manga artist, going so far as to start a middle school manga club. Manga art is derivative in its style as well, imitating and adapting originally from Disney but then self-referencing for the evolution of the form, something on which I have written in the past (c.f. deWinter 2009). In addition to this manga connection, Japanese critics have pointed out that Miyamoto was probably influenced by the children's television show *Hyokkorihyoutanjima* (ひょっこりひょうたん島),

which had a puppet character named Don Gabacho (ドン・ガバチョ)
(Ikeya 2009). Don Gabacho had a big nose, large mustache, and red hat
(albeit a red top hat). So while Mario's name was influenced by a US
landlord whom no one liked, the visual design harkens to this children's
character and a manga aesthetic from Japan. Then, when Miyamoto
started designing *Super Mario Bros.*, he did so around this same character Mario. A lesser known fact, however, is that Miyamoto started to
design Zelda with Mario simultaneously, and Mario was the protagonist of the Zelda game in early drafts. In fact, the game was called *Mario
Adventure* on early design documents ("Bonus Stage 1: Ancient Documents from 1985" n.d.). And this approach to innovation is not unique
to storytelling; evidence of Miyamoto's adaptive innovation can be seen
in Nintendo's hardware evolution as well, and examples of this can be
found in the following section on hardware and software development.

Adaptive innovation supports well this idea of Japanese perfectionism. Miyamoto is often credited with saying "A delayed game is eventually good, a bad game is bad forever." Thus, Nintendo is famous for
its release delays, and among the development community, famous for
its *chabudai gaeshi*, or upending the tea table and scrapping the whole
project. By the time that Nintendo started to develop *Kirby's Adventure* (Nintendo 1993) and *The Legend of Zelda: Ocarina of Time* (1998),
Miyamoto had already moved into a producer position, designing and
directing games only occasionally. However, Miyamoto's perfectionist tendencies, and his love of working on fine-tuning games, can be
seen in his approach to the design and production process of these two
games as well as others. He jokingly (but seriously) said in his 2007
GDC keynote that development teams quake in fear when they hear his
footsteps, afraid that in his producer role, he will upend the tea table.
While these types of stories seem idiosyncratic to a particular story
that we tell of Miyamoto, they are not uncommon in Japan. Indeed,
chabudai gaeshi is a cultural idiom. Further, Japanese perfectionist tendencies are well documented in business literature, with one amusing
story that discusses Japanese manufacturing standards in the 1970s and
1980s. In this story, an American company ordered ball bearings from

a Japanese plant, stipulating that they would accept only twenty defective parts per thousand. The order arrived, and in a separate bag were twenty defective bearings with a note that said, "'We were not sure why you wanted these, but here they are'" (Bolman and Deal 2008, 55). We have luckily not received a similar packet with our games, telling us that these were the bugs that we were expecting in the game.

Business context and early training

When telling the biographical story of his life, people often acknowledge in a throwaway line that Miyamoto has a degree in industrial design. The mythology around Miyamoto tends to emphasize, rather, his artistic nature: he plays banjo and guitar; he likes manga and wants to become a manga artist; he is a long-haired free spirit. And Miyamoto's interviews tend to reinforce these stories. For example, *The New Yorker* "Master of Play" interview article by Nick Paumgarten (2010) emphasizes an idyllic childhood for the free-spirited Miyamoto. He repeats the oft-told story of exploring nature and caves, which gave Miyamoto a sense of wonder in nature—a wonder that he tries to recreate in his games. And while this inspiration is important to understand in his game design process (see Chapter 2 on spatial narratives), also important is his formal training as an industrial engineer.

Industrial engineering is a hybrid field that aims to optimize complex processes or systems through analysis, synthesis, user-testing, prototyping, testing, and implementation with a particular eye to design and human factors. As such, industrial engineers study processes, ergonomics, human factors, psychology, interface design, architecture, engineering, and computer technologies. And finally, because this discipline is closely related to business, training often centers on explicit design strategies and product planning (see, for example, Cross 2008). However, in terms of creative design and style, Michael Tovey (1997) discusses the challenges of communicating style. "Industrial designers," he writes, "employ visual, creative and intuitive techniques in making their special contribution to the design process" (29). And these techniques require designers to train with others in order to discipline their aesthetic tastes (as well as learn the specialized languages of those tastes) and understand the affordances within the technologies.

It is difficult to determine where Shigeru Miyamoto gained his sense of game constraints and affordances. It is certainly true that when he first joined Nintendo, he functionally apprenticed under Gunpei Yokoi, whom Miyamoto credits as the biggest influence on his design career (Schilling 2011).[3] Like many early game designers, Yokoi had a computer-related engineering degree: in his case, electronics. He originally joined Nintendo in 1965 to maintain the *hanafuda* assembly line machines. However, a chance toy design—an extending mechanical arm—caught the attention of the then-president Hiroshi Yamauchi. The Ultra Hand, as it came to be called, was a commercial success, enabling Yokoi to switch to toy design. His eventual transition into a game designer came when he was riding a Shinkansen bullet train and saw a bored businessman punching buttons on his calculator to amuse himself. This event, according to Crigger (2007), inspired Gunpei Yokoi to develop the first Game & Watch game: *Ball* (Nintendo 1980). Game & Watch was a successful product for Nintendo, and the company eventually released fifty-nine titles on this platform.

What is important about Yokoi's Game & Watch development is not so much that he was designing games. Other electrical and computer engineers were also designing games, such as early arcade designers Bushnell and Nolan of Computer Space fame (Bushnell went on to start Atari), Alcorn of Atari, and Ivy from Exidy. Rather, the important contribution that Yokoi had in shaping Miyamoto's designs had to do with Yokoi's attention to both hardware and software to provide an

---

[3] I write "functionally" here because it attends to the more structured approach of mentorship in Japanese society. In Japan, people often belong to a sempai-kohai relationship that is interdependent (see Doi's 1973 discussion of *amae*). People with more experience are *sempai*, and those who are lower in the hierarchy are *kohai*. Both have an obligation to one another. When Miyamoto entered Nintendo, Yokoi assumed a sempai role, supporting and teaching Miyamoto important concepts around the design of computer games.

entertaining experience in the game, discussed earlier in this chapter. And it had to do with him playing games to learn what made them enjoyable and discussing his observations with his mentor Yokoi.

In playing and analyzing games, Miyamoto was adhering to the best practices in industrial design, setting the standard for both aesthetic sensitivity and establishing a baseline for iterative development. Here again, we see the crossover in these categories, strengthened by his industrial design emphasis on iteration in this context; as Cross emphasizes in his text *Engineering Design Models*, "*iteration is a common feature of designing*" (8, emphasis in original). Thus, returning to the example of Jumpman becoming Mario and then being used as the start for early Zelda development, this practice comes as little surprise from someone trained as an industrial designer. Iterative design not only works to bring together large teams to see what works and what doesn't; it also shortens development cycles, which increases a firm's competitive advantage (Clark and Fujimoto 1991; Smith and Eppinger 1997).

In addition to this formal and informal training, Miyamoto learned to design arcade cabinet games first. Good arcades support both the player and the spectator, the assumption being that people would crowd around the game, watch, and comment. In discussing his design process for *Donkey Kong*, for example, Miyamoto said:

> Now, a fun game should always be easy to understand—you should be able to take one look at it and know what you have to do straight away. It should be so well constructed that you can tell at a glance what your goal is and, even if you don't succeed, you'll blame yourself rather than the game. Moreover, the people standing around watching the game have also got to be able to enjoy it. These were the kind of issues I discussed with Yokoi-san. ("Mario Couldn't Jump at First" n.d.)

This early training influenced later game design when games moved to the home console. Miyamoto remained invested in games that create community and interaction, even in such seemingly solitary games as *The Legend of Zelda*. In fact, when he designed *The Legend of Zelda*, he designed it as a game that would get people talking, trading strategies, and building communities. In many ways, Miyamoto showed foresight into the future importance of community management.

Hardware and software development

Miyamoto soon overcame his limited understanding concerning hardware and software. When first designing *Donkey Kong*, for example, Miyamoto had to work closely with Yokoi and software engineers in order to understand what the programs and hardware were capable of; he didn't really have the necessary technological knowledge and abilities at first. He quickly overcame this hurdle, however, and has prided himself on his continued involvement in subsequent hardware design. Miyamoto links his interest in hardware design to his training in industrial design, which is unsurprising considering that industrial design is about the human in technological systems. Nintendo clearly felt that he was insightful since he continued to be involved in the ongoing hardware development. Between the mentoring that he received from Yokoi and his university studies, Miyamoto explained in his GDC keynote "A Creative Vision," "I've been involved in the design of every Nintendo controller on every console since the NES." And here too, we can see the influence of iterative design and innovation based largely on an accident. By this, I once again refer to the first Donkey Kong design for which Miyamoto had to work around an existing control panel (see Figure 1.3).

As can be seen in the top image of Figure 1.3, the original *Radar Scope* had a joystick, 1 and 2 player buttons, and a fire button. The only meaningful change in the production of *Donkey Kong* panel was the relabeling as a jump button rather than a fire button. This simple interface, initially an artifact of a design constraint, meant that people knew the core mechanic of the game and learned to manipulate it quickly. Interestingly, it was Gunpei Yokoi, however, who suggested the arrow pad instead of the joystick, which he included in the Game and Watch release of *Donkey Kong* (see Figure 1.4).

Figure 1.3 *Radar Scope* and *Donkey Kong* control panels.
(Credit: Donald P. Loschiavo, or the Arcadeguy)

Figure 1.4 Game & Watch *Donkey Kong* and the introduction of the D-pad.
(Image retrieved from Wikipedia)

These early developments would influence controller development throughout Nintendo's next thirty-five years with minor adjustments here and there, such as Miyamoto making the "A" button on Nintendo 64's controller larger to indicate that it is the most important button. Miyamoto's influence is not limited to controller hardware; he is often intimately involved in the creation of new consoles as well. And once those consoles are created, it has often fallen to him and his teams to develop software and games that showcase the capabilities of this hardware. A survey of his filed patents provides evidence of this, such as his involvement in developing three-dimensional worlds (US 6155926 A "Video Game System and Method with Enhanced Three-Dimensional Character and Background Control" [2000] or US 6894686 B2 "System and Method for Automatically Editing Capturing Images for Inclusion into 3D Video Game Play" [2005]) or incorporating multiuser communication (see US 6951516 B1 "Method and Apparatus for Multi-User Communications Using Discrete Video Game Platforms" [2005]), and even the ability to save games and transfer the saved data to other platforms (US 6132315 A "Game System Operable with Backup Data on Different Kinds of Game Machines" [2000]). An interesting note should be added here: it is this ability to "save" games that harkens back to his early days' designing. *The Legend of Zelda* (1986) was the first game on a home console that would allow the player to save the game, enabling Miyamoto to design an immersive experience that took many days to complete. He did this by including an internal battery in the cartridge and saving the game directly on that cartridge. Loguidice and Barton (2009) credit this innovation with closing the gap between consoles and home computers.

Experience design and storytelling

The final category concerns the games themselves and what he has designed into those games. First and foremost, Miyamoto is credited with introducing narrative structure into a game. Now this might be debatable depending on where a person stands concerning narrative structure. For example, *Space Invaders*—the game that inspired Miyamoto before he became a game designer—can be said to have narrative structure. The aliens start to invade Earth. The protagonist player must defend earth in never-ending conflict. However, what Miyamoto gave the player were motivations and narrative connections between each scene. *Donkey Kong*, for example, starts with the gorilla taking Lady away, which sets up the conflict. Each level is connected to the last via the narrative (Donkey Kong takes Lady and escapes from Jumpman). From the beginning, Miyamoto brought narrative into the games that he designed. In an interview concerning narratives and stories in games, Miyamoto explained, "I have been a big fan of comics since I was a young boy and so one idea I had in creating that game was to apply a little bit of story to it in order to help people understand the concepts of the game better. It was a similar way to what you see with comics" ("Miyamoto: The Interview" 2007). In this, Miyamoto is often credited with a cinematic approach to game design. He dismisses these praises, explaining that some people have told him that he should try directing film, but he laughs such suggestions off ("Conference Keynote" 1999).

In addition to these observations concerning narrative, I would add that one of Miyamoto's contributions to game design is his use of space in narratives. In *Donkey Kong*, each level is part of a continued narrative tied together. This connectedness of levels remains true through the Super Mario games and becomes especially apparent in Zelda. In fact, Zelda's narrative is almost all spatial, requiring the player to unfold the story only by going to certain areas. In this, Zelda breaks away from Miyamoto's earlier designs in that the demands of the game are not always immediately apparent but only unfold via interaction with the storyline. In a 2003 interview with *Super Play Magazine*, Miyamoto reflected back on Zelda: "I remember that we were very nervous, because *The Legend of Zelda* was our first game that forced the players to think about what they should do next. We were afraid that gamers would become bored and stressed by the new concept" ("Super Play Magazine interviews"). With this narrative structure, Miyamoto and the development team were breaking new ground on what games could do, and ultimately the home console market embraced this new approach to games and storytelling.

While Miyamoto is famous for storytelling, his own self-professed interest is in experience design—he wants gamers to have a fun and entertaining experience, one that is often social. This can probably be seen best in *Super Mario Kart* (Nintendo 1992) and subsequent work. *Super Mario Kart* has no real narrative structure. Instead, it uses characters from the Mario universe to create a fun racing game that people enjoy playing in multiplayer mode. In fact, *Mario Kart's* main contribution is its multiplayer mode, which was noted in the reviews that accompanied its release in *Nintendo Power* as well as retrospective reviews online. *Mario Kart* is fun, fast, and silly. Videos of people playing *Mario Kart* games on YouTube, for example, always show people laughing, praising the game, and trying to strategize how to use power-ups against their friends and family in funny ways. While other racing games might focus competition on winning (think *Pole Position*, Namco/Atari, 1982), Mario Kart balances this motivation with the experience of family fun for all ages. This emphasis on experience over narrative becomes even more prevalent in later games, such as *Nintendogs* (Nintendo 2005), which offers players a cute simulation of dog ownership without any of the negative experiences often associated with real-life pets.

In fact, there is a strange quotation from Miyamoto that emphasizes his commitment to experience over narrative or art, and it has to do with female and gay avatars. Miyamoto was responding in an interview, which referenced sexism in games.[4] Miyamoto explained: "So, if we end up creating a gameplay structure where it makes sense for, whether it's a female to go rescue a male or a gay man to rescue a lesbian woman or a lesbian woman to rescue a gay man, we might take that approach. For us it's less about the story and more about the structure of the gameplay

---

[4] Miyamoto was probably asked this question because the gaming community shone a spotlight on sexism in games with the "Tropes vs. Women" documentary by Anita Sarkeesian and the near simultaneous #1reasonwhy for the Twitter discussion.

and what makes sense to be presenting to the consumer" (Cook 2013). Such a response is, of course, problematic because it ignores powerful choices that are made in the structure of the game, even if the emphasis is on gameplay. However, what this quotation seeks to highlight is the emphasis that Miyamoto places on experience over narrative in his self-defined design vision. Thus, Dymek's assertion that "the 'narratives' of Miyamoto's games are ornamental at best, or childishly primitive at worst—the focus is without a doubt on the gameplay" (2010, 425), while somewhat pejorative, echoes much of what Miyamoto believes of his own game design work. When discussing *The Legend of Zelda*, he has famously stated that he is more interested in gameplay than narrative, asking his development team to cut back on the narrative elements. In the serial interview feature on Nintendo.com entitled Iwata Asks, the current president Satoru Iwata interviewed Miyamoto, saying: "You would rather spend your energy making game elements rather than the story" to which Miyamoto responded "That's right" ("Everyone Loves Horses" n.d.). Yet legions of fans and game designers see his influence on the narratives of games, often heralding them as some of the best in game history.

In both his narrative and experience designs, what draws his work together is an extreme attention to detail concerning the entire immersive environment. This includes visuals, music, animations, controls, story, game mechanics, and so forth. While I discuss these at length in subsequent chapters in relation to individual games, it is worth noting that, from very early on, Miyamoto emphasized that complete games were only as good as the polish on component parts. Indeed, many of his interviews have discussed the long polishing periods dedicated to his games. Some of this attention to detail has to do with Japanese perfectionism, but as Iwata explores in one of his interviews with Miyamoto, some of this has to do with Miyamoto's eclectic interests when he was younger. In a conversation concerning Miyamoto's early influences in music, Iwata observed, "It's fascinating. If you hadn't experienced music in so many different ways, you might never have made some of the games that you have. For example, you might not have paid as much attention to the music in the Mario games, and Wii Music might never have been made at all" ("Shigeru Miyamoto's Early Encounters with Music" n.d.). Shigeru Miyamoto's early interests were artistic, his later training was as an engineer in systems, and these come together to bring us games that stand on their individual components and as a whole.

"I have enjoyed creating something that is unique, something others have not done"[5]

In 2007, *Time Magazine* listed Miyamoto in its list of one hundred most influential people (Wendel 2007), and the following year, Miyamoto was the number one choice of a people's vote for one hundred most influential people in a *Time Magazine* Poll (Brown and Kung 2008). As of 2013, Miyamoto was discussing the new, yet unnamed franchise that he intended to create. Meanwhile, rumors abound about his impending retirement. Miyamoto himself has said in a recent interview that he is preparing for the day that he will retire: "Instead, what we're doing internally is, on the assumption that there may someday be a time when I'm no longer there, and in order for the company to prepare for that, what I'm doing is pretending like I'm not working on half the projects that I would normally be working on to try to get the younger staff to be more involved" (Madden 2013). Regardless of whether he will retire in the short term or release a new franchise, the influence of Shigeru Miyamoto over the last forty years is undeniable. This book, then, is a consideration of that influence.

Before delving into individual chapters, I do want to note a challenge concerning organization. One way to organize this book is around design categories that I have identified and explained in this chapter, giving each a full treatment. However, because each of these often

---

[5] This Miyamoto quotation comes from a 2007 interview with Anjali Rao ("Shigeru Miyamoto Talk Asia Interview").

informs the other during the design of a single game, the limitations become immediately visible. Another approach is to attend to single, very influential games and carefully give treatment to those. I will do this, yet I necessarily must add to this. To treat only individual games is to ignore the significant back and forth between games and design elements that affect single games simultaneously. For example, Miyamoto started work on *Super Mario Bros.* and *The Legend of Zelda* at the same time, yet *Zelda* was released a full year later because of the specific development demands of that game. Thus, it is useful to talk about the design of these two games in tandem. This lends itself to an era approach, which I will heavily rely on, diverging only to make certain points concerning long-term design vision and action. And this is why I will not organize under franchises—that is, the Mario franchise or Zelda franchise, for example. While these share common characters and sometimes narrative elements, they belong to different moments in hardware and software histories, and thus the gameplay and experiences are not consistent across the years. Ultimately, my purpose is to paint a picture of a game auteur, one who designs unique games that attract a wide-ranging player-audience, one who designs experiences for fun, and one who helps us to remember that "inside every adult is the heart of a child" (Miyamoto, qtd in Sayre 2007).

2

Spatial Narratives: Characters in their Worlds

Early in the history of video games, arcade cabinets offered players a series of discrete game boards. For example, *Asteroids* (Atari 1979) provides the player with a single screen in which a player controls a triangular ship that must shoot asteroids into smaller and smaller chunks without getting hit. Or for a more complex game, consider *Pac-Man* (Namco 1980), a game that Miyamoto holds in high regard as one of his favorite games. *Pac-Man* provides players with a series of discrete mazes through which the player must navigate, eating balls, avoiding ghosts, and eating power balls to be able to eat those same ghosts. While this game does provide players with multiple levels, each is separate from the other. In fact, other than an imperative to live and clear boards, narrative was not introduced into the Pac-Man universe until the 1982 release of *Ms. Pac-Man* (Bally Midway, Namco), and the narrative was encapsulated in cut scenes between maze types: "They meet," "The chase," and "Junior." I do not want to dismiss this evolution in gaming history; *Ms. Pac-Man* is the first game to use cut scenes. However, the levels that players progressed to were still isolated. Meanwhile, in the home console market, *Adventure* (Atari 1979) provided the player with a map game in which players had to collect keys, fight dragons, and solve mazes. Yet this game was criticized for rudimentary graphics and unbalanced challenge over the course of gameplay. And it is here that Miyamoto's games helped to shape the industry: He provided games that were spatially connected to provide players with an integrated play experience that was visually polished and accessible for both short and long play sessions.

In this chapter, I examine Miyamoto's use of space and maps to create narratives, build worlds for characters, and provide players with challenging play experiences. In the history of video games, I argue, this evolution in the use of narratives shaped the types of stories that games provide players, creating spaces for exploration and surprise. Indeed, in responding to an interview question concerning the secret to a great game, Miyamoto says: "I think it has to do with balance. My formula for success is that 70 percent of the game should have to do with objectives, and the rest should be secrets and exploration—things such as burning trees to find a hidden dungeon entrance link in the first Zelda game" ("The Legend of Miyamoto" 1998, 52). This spatial formation creates two types of narratives in Miyamoto's games (and subsequent games influenced by this approach). The first is a narrative that unfolds as players progress linearly through the game, such as *Donkey Kong* (Nintendo 1981) or the side-scrolling variants of the Mario games. The second is a narrative that is layered with both linearity as defined by objectives (find the hidden key) as well as nonlinear idiosyncratic play that each gamer introduces into the unfolding of the plot. The nonlinear play allows for different experiences of space because players traverse the map in their own ways, different emotions that can include boredom, frustration, joy, or optimism because of how players are able to navigate or interpret challenges, or different amounts of time on task because of luck or skill.

What holds these games together is not a series of levels that are connected only through a high score (although the leader board is still there with some of the games, so this does still play a role); it is the flow between each level, a purposeful movement through space. While Miyamoto often uses the analogy of playgrounds or nature, he does spend time talking about building worlds that make sense to characters. In other words, he creates characters that have special abilities and then he creates environments that make sense for that character (Mario can jump, so the world includes platforms for jumping, for example). We see this again and again in Miyamoto's franchises, such as Donkey Kong, Mario, Zelda, Kirby, and even Pikmin and Nintendogs. This type of world building, further, can account for the types of player immersion and personal investment that players often felt in games like *The Legend of Zelda*, a game in which players slowly unfold the story through the process of spatial exploration—a topic that I will take up later in this chapter. First, however, I turn to *Donkey Kong* to explore an early example of this linked landscape.

Donkey Kong and climbing the building

In Chapter 1, I discussed *Donkey Kong* at some length, partially because it is part of what enabled Miyamoto to become a game designer and partly because it is the first example that encompasses many of his design practices. I will take this game up again here to consider the beginning of spatial storytelling. When Miyamoto was originally given the challenge of converting the *Radar Scope* (1979) cabinets, he conceived of *Donkey Kong* as a side-scrolling game. However, the hardware that was available in the *Rader Scope* cabinets would not support side scrolling. This material limitation required some rethinking of the original design so that the eventual *Donkey Kong* would be comprised of four screens that represented different 25-meter levels of a steel structural building, making the total building 100 meters tall. Interestingly, Miyamoto's team also had to figure out what to do with the "Fire" button on the *Radar Scope* cabinet. In an Iwata Asks interview, Miyamoto explained that they created a scenario that asked what a character would do if a barrel were coming toward it. The answer: Jump. Without that extraneous button, Jumpman would probably not have jumped (in fact, early in development, he was called Mr Video because he still lacked the ability to jump) ("Mario Couldn't Jump at First" n.d.).

The question then raised was what goal would make sense for Jumpman, and the answer was to go up. While early iterations of the game experimented with mazes (probably inspired by Miyamoto's respect for *Pac-Man* and the market success of that same game), the team eventually abandoned that because of the difficulty of marrying jumping with mazes. Thus, the team decided to make Jumpman climb. In this final product, we can see the combination of space with narrative. When players approach the game, they are greeted by the high-score page, indicating that scores are the win condition for the game. True to form, winning can be evaluated only on the basis of player score; there is no win screen, no complete game.

The game starts with a clear call to action within a game narrative. What I mean by this is that some games start and have the player figure out what needs to be done whereas others tell the player to complete a task in writing on the screen. Almost all arcade games provide an objective and directions for gameplay on the cabinet itself as a paratext to the video game. In *Donkey Kong*, the player puts a quarter in to start the game and then is greeted by sinister-sounding music, reminiscent of early cinema organ music used to identify the antagonist. Donkey Kong takes Lady and climbs a ladder up to the top of the screen, puts Lady down at the very top, and jumps to break the ladders. Then the screen prompts the player: "How high can you get?" with a meter-based measurement offered. In Figure 2.1, I describe each level with its corresponding image. The levels are inverted, however, to recreate the tower, with level one at the bottom and level four at the top.

Throughout playing the game, Lady calls for help, and Donkey Kong is obviously trying to thwart the player. The love triangle acts to provide rudimentary motivation within the storyline, and the player has a clear narrative role as the protagonist. This is not an original storyline, however; *Donkey Kong* is at best a simple adaptation of the Popeye storyline that Miyamoto was originally planning—Popeye, Olive Oyl, and Bluto. What Miyamoto carefully recreated in these characters was a sense of comedy. The Donkey Kong character—a large and goofy ape—is not scary and wasn't intended to be scary. This is why this same character can appear in other games as a playable character or part of a team. Miyamoto even wanted the name to be

Screen 4 (all the way up to 100 meters): In the long fall level, the visuals let players know that they are at the top of the building: the beams taper off into a triangle. The purpose of this level is to remove the rivets so that Donkey Kong falls from the building, all the while avoiding the flames that stalk the level. Lady and Jumpman are reunited at the end with a heart over their heads. And then the game starts over again.

Screen 3 (meters 51–75): This time, Jumpman must avoid pies (or coal) rolling on conveyor belts, climb ladders, and move through those same conveyor belts to get to Lady. One last time, Donkey Kong runs with Lady.

Screen 2 (meters 26–50): Jumpman starts on a platform surrounded by elevators. He must get to the top once again by using a combination of ladders and elevators. He must avoid getting crushed between an elevator and the platform and still manage to avoid fireballs. Again, when he reaches the top, Donkey Kong climbs with Lady again.

Screen 1 (the first 25 meters): Jumpman starts at the bottom and must go up seven stories of sloped steel beams and ladders to get to Lady. Meanwhile, Donkey Kong throws barrels, which can kill Jumpman if they come in contact. Further, the barrels can burn in oil, which releases fireballs that chase Jumpman. Jumpman can get the hammer and score extra points by destroying barrels. The level ends when Jumpman reaches the top and Donkey Kong grabs Lady to climb up to the next level.

Figure 2.1 Donkey Kong levels, showing the vertically spatial storyline and gameplay.

familiar yet whimsical as well. He chose Donkey because donkeys are stubborn and Kong because of the obvious similarities with King Kong. In many ways, this invokes multimedia intertextuality with two other established intellectual properties, adapting them for new uses, again common in Japanese business practices. As *Donkey Kong* ascended in popularity, Universal Studios clearly did not share an affinity for this sort of adaptation, and the company filed suit against Nintendo for *King Kong* trademark infringement ("King Kong Toppled" 1984, 19). Universal eventually lost the suit even though the King Kong reference is there to see. However, the experience of the game is not like the movie. The movie is about fear and saving the girl whereas *Donkey Kong* is not just about getting the girl; it's about the action of climbing the skyscraper to get the girl.

What can be seen in this initial game is a foreshadowing of Miyamoto's early design work, and some of this may be accidental because of the limitations placed on the original *Donkey Kong* design. Had Miyamoto been able to design a game that was a series of mazes like *Pac-Man* or a sidescroller like *Pitfall* (Arari 1982), he may not have imagined a vertical map. The narrative movement through space, furthermore, provides rising action, in this case literally. In *Donkey Kong*, we can see evidence of the most basic form of cinematic three-act structure, with a call to action, rising action with a series of reversals, and resolution (Trottier 2014). While Kohler claims that *Donkey Kong* is the first game to tell a narrative story from beginning to end (or from bottom to top), I would argue that what we see here is the narrative being used to outline the objectives in a way that is cinematically integrated into the video interface. And cinema matters to Miyamoto, as I will discuss later in this chapter. Thus, as Miyamoto moves into *Super Mario Bros.* (Nintendo 1983) and *The Legend of Zelda* (Nintendo 1984), this practice of using spatial narratives to immerse players and provide the player with objectives and experiences is refined, defining two of the most successful franchises for Nintendo and embedding a place for Zelda and Mario in the hearts of video game players the world over.

Mario and Zelda: Exploring spaces as a core game mechanic

It may seem strange initially to speak about Zelda and Mario in the same section, especially considering that these are generically two different games—one is a sidescroller and the other is an adventure game. However, Miyamoto started working with his teams to start designing these games simultaneously, and Miyamoto has explained that designs from one game turned up in another, and that both games had similar design visions. Miyamoto continued to work closely with Gunpei Yokoi, but for the design and eventual roll out of these two titles, Miyamoto's close collaborators were Takashi Tezuka, who also did not have a background in game design before joining Nintendo, and Toshihiko Nakago, who worked with Miyamoto on *Excitebike* (Nintendo 1984). President Iwata has referred to these three designers, Miyamoto, Tezuka, and Nakago, as the "golden triangle" because so many of the games that they collaborate on go on to be huge successes ("It Started with a Square Object Moving," n.d.).

Writing about game designers as single auteurs with a vision is often difficult because game designers usually work closely with others, including producers who have design input, codirectors, teams of designers, and even hardware designers. Within the old documents released by Nintendo, it is often difficult to identify Miyamoto's work outside of his collaborations. This is fine because it speaks to his process as a designer and one that he admits to often. For example, when asked where he gets design ideas, Miyamoto has said, "I wish I could find somewhere where I could get ideas, but unfortunately, I don't have any specific place. Rather, in my case, I often come up with ideas while I am talking with my programmers and creators" (Fielder 1999). It comes as no surprise, then, that when President Iwata shows an old design map during the interview, Nakago reminisces about watching Miyamoto and Tezuka sitting side by side, drawing simultaneously on the same map ("Bonus Stage 1" n.d.).

Within these two later games, *Super Mario Bros.* and *The Legend of Zelda*, Miyamoto started imagining character and abilities and the designed worlds that would suit those characters. This is an extension of what he did in *Donkey Kong* in which he imagined a game board that would best suit a jumping man. The character and the gameplay affordances made possible by those characters affected the world building, which in turn affected other character creations. Throughout, these two early games are somewhat dreamlike and surreal in presentation as Russel DeMaria notes in the documentary *The Videogame Revolution* (Palmer 2004). Each game refers back in some way to childhood spaces: the playground for *Super Mario Bros.* and the woods and caves that Miyamoto whiled away time in, Sonobe, for *Zelda*. Each game is multilayered, and each hides surprises in space. Thus, a player who revisits levels and spaces multiple times is rewarded. Before delving into examples of these, I turn to the characters of these two games.

Super Mario Bros.

It was never preplanned that Link and Mario would appear as the protagonists of two of Nintendo's most important brands. When the development teams got together, they had to design for the 1983 Famicom (known in the United States as the Nintendo Entertainment System). What the development team knew was that they needed to design a game that utilized the hardware available, and the hardware for the Famicom would adapt the D-pad controller input from the Game & Watch series rather than the joystick of the arcade or Atari 2600. The team started designing a square that moved around in space for the *Super Mario* game using the D-pad for directional input, but the movement enabled eventually would inform *The Legend of Zelda* ("Using the D-pad to Jump"). For the Mario game, the team wanted "a dynamic, athletic kind of game that would be set on land, sea and air and that would feature a large character" ("It Started with a Square Object Moving") while Zelda was meant to be more about exploration. Even though the dynamic movement that would eventually be Zelda was groundbreaking, it did not convey the core concept of the game. For this, Miyamoto used Jumpman—now Mario.

Mario was chosen early in the design process of both *Super Mario Bros.* and *The Legend of Zelda* because the brand proved to be commercially successful. In an interview with President Iwata, Tezuka spoke specifically to this point, explaining that he went over to the head of the Sales and Marketing Division and asked to see sales numbers (amazing considering that he had been with the company for only one year). He looked at the numbers and saw that the *Mario Bros.* (1983) game that Miyamoto designed initially for arcade release continued to sell well on the Famicom one year later. *Mario Bros.* followed the release of *Donkey Kong, Donkey Kong Jr.* (1982), and *Popeye* (1982), adapting many of the ideas that Miyamoto used in platformer games ("It Started with a Square Object Moving").

Mario's abilities morphed during these early game iterations. Because of his close working relationship with Yokoi, Miyamoto was convinced by his mentor to allow Mario to fall from great heights without getting hurt—something that Miyamoto was dubious about because he thought that wasn't realistic. *Mario Bros.* also introduced the game mechanic of hitting turtles from underneath and then knocking them away. The knocking away added a level of challenge that wasn't there when all a player had to do was attack from below. In developing *Super Mario Bros.*, the team wanted to have a large Mario jumping around the screen. They eventually opted to have a magic mushroom that would enable the character to grow big and maintain Mario's ability to fall without getting hurt ("The Man Behind Mario" 1991). And Mario could still jump.

With this character in mind, Miyamoto and his team started level designs for his games, and documents and photos that are contemporary of that time show Miyamoto drawing a series of maps for horizontal worlds that Mario could run through, keeping the heart of a fun and energetic game (these can be found throughout Nintendo magazines and on Iwata Asks interviews). However, these were not just horizontal worlds, as can be seen in Figure 2.2, a composite image made up of screenshots strung together. Miyamoto hand-drew these maps in the design process and then implemented them.

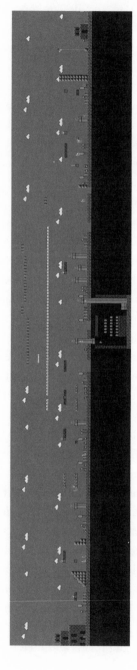

Figure 2.2 *Super Mario Bros.*'s world map of level 2.1 showing underground level and sky level. *(Screenshot and original composite credit: Ian Albert [http://ian-albert.com/games/super_mario_bros_maps/] Additional image composite credit: Aaron McGaffey)*

What can be seen right away is the secret levels that can be found only through exploration.

As can be seen, a person can run through the level, following a linear narrative arc: Start running, don't die, and try again and again to save Princess Toadstool, otherwise known as Princess Peach, from the evil clutches of Bowser. We know the narrative because the book that accompanies the game tells us. The object of the game is not to win, the booklet informs us. Rather, it relies on the narrative for its call to action:

> One day the kingdom of the peaceful mushroom people was invaded by Koopa, a tribe of turtles famous for their black magic. The quiet, peace-loving Mushroom people were turned into mere stones, bricks and even field horse-hair plants, and the Mushroom Kingdom fell into ruin.
>
> The only one who can undo the magic spell on the Mushroom People and return them to their normal selves is the Princess Toadstool, the daughter of the Mushroom King. Unfortunately, she is presently in the hands of the great Koopa turtle king.
>
> Mario, the hero of the story (maybe) hears about the Mushroom People's plight and sets out on a quest to free the Mushroom Princess from the evil Koopa and restore the fallen kingdom of the Mushroom People.
>
> You are Mario! It's up to you to save the Mushroom People from the black magic of the Koopa! (*Super Mario Bros. Booklet* 1985, 2)

This game focuses on a hero's call to adventure rather than on winning points. Picking up the controller is the moment that the player crosses the threshold to start training, to "maybe" become the hero. This should be a linear call, with tests and setbacks. And it can be. But the space available in *Super Mario Bros.*, the space that Miyamoto created, is more playful, often diverging away from the narrative while still serving it with forced directions and timers. Further, this structure had tremendous influence across the gaming industry.

Many people find it difficult to remember playing the first *Super Mario Bros.* and not knowing about the secret pipes and spaces in midair that would release a vine for climbing, yet the magazines from the 1980s attest to the fact that players did not always know of the secrets hidden in the game. Questions and advice range from "Where are the warp zones in Super Mario Bros. and how do I get to them?" ("Counselor's Corner" 1988, 66) to "How to get to the hidden room in World 3-1" ("Pro's Corner" 1987, 20). Indeed, when *Super Mario Bros. 3* was released, *Nintendo Power* dedicated all of volume 13's content to a strategy guide for the game (*Nintendo Power Strategy Guide* 1990). No other material was covered and no contests were run. While I will speak to challenge in the next chapter, the point here is that the use of space was different, mysterious, and fun, breaking the linearity of objective-based gameplay but not subverting it completely. Here, Miyamoto's analogy of a playground may be used to make sense of these design choices.

Miyamoto often talks about his childhood as providing a firm starting point for his design processes. When asked about his ongoing philosophy about making video games, Miyamoto responded, "I think great video games are like favorite playgrounds, places you become attached to and go back to again and again. Wouldn't it be great to have a whole drawer full of 'playgrounds' right at your finger tips?" ("The Man Behind Mario" 1991, 32). These feelings are well encapsulated in *Super Mario Bros.* and subsequent Mario titles. The colors are bright and attractive. The environment promotes climbing and jumping, and even in underwater levels, the sense of buoyancy is lively. Every time players go in, they can choose to include different aspects into the game. They can choose to warp from one part of the map to another, traversing representational space and opting into a shorter game experience. They can try again and again to get the jump just right on the turtle at the end of World 3-1 to get a large number of free lives. They can explore every part of the world. Thus, when Jenkins (1998) explores childhood cultures and the connections between playgrounds and video games, his analysis is based in large part on Miyamoto's influence on the game industry, interpreting playgrounds into play spaces.

In addition to providing a playground for players, *Super Mario Bros.* is a replayable game. The purpose of the game is not to find out what the end is. In other words, the motive to play is not diminished once the player knows the full storyline. This is a game that shifts the locus of challenge from the game (there is no easy, normal, or hard setting on this game) to the player. As Greg Costinkyan (2013) notes in his book *Uncertainty in Games*, "Super Mario Bros. is practically the Platonic ideal of what game designers call a 'player-skill' (as opposed to 'character-skill') game [that perfect standard that all other copies attempt to achieve]. Luck is not a factor. Strategic thinking is not relevant. Puzzle solving is rarely germane. Success is virtually 100 percent dependent on your mastery of the controls, and your ability to respond to the situation unfolding on your screen with accuracy and alacrity" (20). In his chapter "Everything I Know About Game Design I Learned from Super Mario Bros." Curry backs up this claim and builds on it. According to Curry, this early game had all of the essential elements of game design, making it "the most influential videogame of all time" (n.d.). Without it, he argues, we may not have had such seminal games as *Metroid* (Nintendo 1996), *Sonic the Hedgehog* (Sonic Team 1991), or *Crash Bandicoot* (Naughty Dog 1996).

The Legend of Zelda

While Mario was about playing in the structure of playgrounds, *The Legend of Zelda* developed around a core concept of free exploration, linking discovery to the core narrative of the game. *Zelda* came out a full year after *Super Mario Bros.* even though production was started on them simultaneously (and even though *Zelda* was ahead of *Super Mario Bros.* at one stage of development). Early design ideas for *Zelda* attempted to exploit the Disk System's ability to rewrite data onto the cartridge (Miyamoto 2011, 2).[1] Development continued, and the decision was made to make this a story-driven game. Slightly more than a year after its Japan release on the Disk System, *Zelda* was released to the US market on a cartridge with an internal battery, which enabled saving for the first time on cartridge-based games.

---

[1]   The Disk System is a Nintendo game system that looked more like a PC, complete with a floppy drive.

The Legend of Zelda is a groundbreaking game, and this mostly has to do with challenge. The booklet that introduces the game provides a narrative backdrop that is legendary in tone. Like *Super Mario Bros.*, the kingdom was invaded by an evil magician—Ganon—and like *Super Mario Bros.*, the player must rescue the princess who can return everything to normal. At the end of this textual call to adventure is this phrase: "Can Link really destroy Ganon and save princess Zelda? Only your skill can answer that question. Good luck. Use the Triforce wisely" (*The Legend of Zelda Booklet* 1986, 4). The book then provides the player with a series of hints that compel the player to explore, such as asking her how many labyrinths she has found and suggestions that hints will be provided to solve riddles. Then the imperative: "Don't rush forward too fast! It's dangerous" (8). The game begins, and the player is prompted to put his or her name into the main board so that the cartridge can store the information. This use of storage is a significant advancement in games, allowing players to walk away and then return to continue the same game. More importantly, the storing of the player's progress allowed Miyamoto and his design team to design a complicated game that didn't assume an unskilled and potentially lazy player but assumed that the player would take the time and invest the energy to move forward.

Miyamoto admitted that, at first, he was concerned about the complexity of the game, thinking that it would turn players off of the title. In reminiscing about the release of *The Legend of Zelda* in 2003, Miyamoto explained, "*The Legend of Zelda* was our first game that forced the players to think about what they should do next. We were afraid that gamers would become bored and stressed by the new concept. Luckily, they reacted the total opposite. It was these elements that made the game so popular, and today gamers tell us how fun the *Zelda* riddles are, and how happy they become when they've solved a task and proceeded with the adventure" ("Super Play Magazine Interviews" 2003). These riddles depend mostly on spatial exploration, which drew on Miyamoto's cave adventures from his childhood. He would go out into nature and explore, playing in the densely growing woods. When he discovered a cave, he spent a great deal of time exploring it thoroughly.

Thus, when design for *Zelda* began, early documents indicated that it would be a dungeon crawler game. But the team eventually moved it to be multileveled and include aboveground and belowground elements (much like *Mario*). Also, while this is an adventure game, complete with sword throwing and weapons collecting, it is at heart an exploration and problem-solving game.

So many of the puzzles in *The Legend of Zelda* are spatial challenges—finding items in one space (often hidden) and applying those items in another space. Then, once down in the dungeons, the map becomes an element of gameplay, constantly present in the top left corner of the screen (see Figure 2.3).

This game was complicated enough that the *Tips and Tactics* strategy guide was available almost immediately after its initial release, offering more comprehensive maps (but not giving away the ending) and walk-throughs of the puzzles. Perusing old issues of *Nintendo Fan Club News* and *Nintendo Power*, it is interesting to see the number of letters and columns that were dedicated to helping players with the spatial puzzles and cluing in the players to other spaces they may not have known about. One particularly amusing letter appears in a 1988 *Nintendo Fan Club News* Mail Bag section. In it, Marilyn Lee Reed writes:

Dear Nintendo, This year we acquired the Nintendo Entertainment System with your Super Mario Bros. cartridge. After noticing what great fun Jeff (age 30) was having with this machine, I rushed out

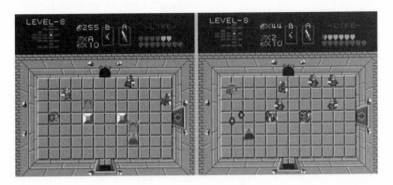

Figure 2.3 Screenshot of *The Legend of Zelda* level 8 dungeon.

to purchase The Legend of Zelda. Since then, Jeff has spoken at the most, six words; his sleeping habits have gone from a normal eight hours to quick cat naps. . . . My husband needs some sort of advice (or map) indicating how to get out of castle five (or is it six?) and into eight (or is it nine?) and on to Death Mountain to rescue this chick called Zelda—fast! While the world is rescuing Zelda, you wonderful people are going to have to rescue Jeff! Please hurry. ("Mail Bag" 1988, 26)

In this letter (and many others besides), we see evidence of a key Miyamoto outcome—and one that I will take up later in this book at more length—and that's collaboration. In *Mario*, collaboration could be achieved through multiplayer mode, much like arcade games. *Zelda* appears to be a single-player game, forcing player isolation. However, Miyamoto has explained that he wanted people to go to work and talk about the game, share tips, and build community through communication about experiences. This letter evidences spouses talking but also people reaching out to a broader community—this is a game that is difficult to win without help.

In addition to spatial puzzles, this game is an excellent early example of the type of in-game narrative that Jenkins and Squire (2002) discuss—narratives that are spatially constructed rather than linearly constructed: "Game designers use spatial elements to set the initial terms for the player's experiences. Information essential to the story is embedded in objects such as books, carved runes or weapons. Artifacts such as jewels may embody friendship or rivalries or may become magical sources of the player's power. The game space is organized so that paths through the game world guide or constrain action, making sure we encounter characters or situations critical to the narrative" (70). Of course, these encounters happen. The story unravels as players navigate Link to find objects, collect and spend money, and defeat monsters. The story is the same for everyone—the game ends only when the player collects the three pieces of the Triforce—yet different for each player—the game unravels over different periods of time and in different orders. It is the difference that matters because it is what creates the bond between the players and Link and also what allows story spaces to become places of adventure.

In creating bonds between players and Link, Miyamoto may have unconsciously tapped into Campbell's idea of the Hero's Journey (2008). In this, the hero is part of an ordinary world; he doesn't even have a sword. In taking up the sword in the game, the player is taking up the challenge and shifting from an innocent child to one who must learn the rules and triumph over a series of trials. These trials need the player to be involved, solving puzzles and riddles. This is not a game that a player can win by mashing a button and eventually killing all of the enemies on the screen. Rather, the player must fight and dodge, explore and reexplore, and solve puzzles. This all acts to ensure that the player is an integral part of this world. She doesn't have the ability to save the world—that is up to Princess Zelda—but she can learn how to control Link and use her wits to traverse the map and defeat Ganon. Furthermore, if these games were easy, the probable immersion would be less. Rather, because the player has to invest so much time and intellectual engagement into the world, she is more likely to think about the game when not playing (think about the husband in the letter above). Success comes only after toil, which makes that success all the more sweet. This toil is not capricious, based on luck and whatever fates are programed into the algorithm. There is a logic to it that rewards the player. Miyamoto spoke specifically to this in relation to another game: *Link's Crossbow Training* (Nintendo 2007). He explained:

> The fact is, the journey is really the reward. And there are times when game creators use well-made "rewards" as the excuse. For example, if someone invents an ending that they're really proud of, that they just think is fantastic, then they might end up settling for a less-than-splendid journey. But that's a definite case of getting your priorities mixed up. So with Link's Crossbow Training, I really saw it as my responsibility to make sure that the creators didn't get too caught up with the reward, and focus instead on making the journey itself the fun part. I even told them not to make any bosses. ("The 'Process' as the Reward")

The games are not about the resolution or the return with the hero's elixir. They are about the actions, the journey, and the time spent doing things in a world. Experiencing frustration and overcoming it through skill and practice are more rewarding than a well-crafted ending.

In addition to the connections between the player and Link is the connection between the player and the setting of Hyrule as a place. Here too, we can see Miyamoto's influence on the trajectory of video games: Miyamoto provides players with open space to play in while also providing the closed places that are defined by the narratives. Consider Michel De Certeau's (1984) argument that stories are spatial metaphors: "Stories could also take this noble name [metaphorai]: every day, they traverse and organize places; they select and link them together; they make sentences and itineraries out of them. They are spatial trajectories" (115). Stories, De Certeau emphasizes, fix space as a culturally creative act (123). Likewise, Yi-Fu Tuan (1977) explores the idea of fixing place in opposition to the openness of space: "The ideas 'space' and 'place' require each other for definition. From the security and stability of place we are aware of the openness, freedom, and threat of space, and vice versa. Furthermore, if we think of space as that which allows movement, then place is pause; each pause in movement makes it possible for location to be transformed into place" (6). In other words, places are defined by something happening in a space, and that something fixes space both geographically and temporally: "That's the place where I proposed marriage." Or more germane to this game, "That's the place where I found the second Triforce or got stuck for five hours."

The balance that *The Legend of Zelda* managed to achieve was to provide the player with both a sense of cultural place and a sense of personal place. The sense of personal place is easier to see. These are the places in the game where I as the player have done something idiosyncratic to my game, such as always dying or feeling the elation of finding something after searching for a long time. In this, my time playing the game stories my personal experiences into the world; I would be narrativizing myself into the game space. These game experiences become my experiences. In many ways, this affinity is formed through the gameplay, the affordances of what I am able to do to complement the plot, which is the role of a good relationship between gameplay and narrative (see Juul 2005). Such a relationship may help to understand Miyamoto's position on narratives as a whole. Often, he is quoted as not caring about narratives, that his main focus is on gameplay only. Yet this is not completely true. In a *Super Play Magazine* interview, Miyamoto discussed narrative in the Zelda universe, explaining, "The most important thing for me, is the player get sucked into the game. I want the games to be easy to understand, and that the people appreciate the game's content, its core. I will never deny the importance of a great story, but the plot should never get that important that it becomes unclear" ("Super Play Magazine Interviews" 2003). The clarity comes from the play experience, the ability to explore, and the joy of discovery. The narrative is there to provide objectives. Further, the narrative helps to shape a sense of community place.

Community places are those places that are storied for those connected to events, culture, and history. These are the places where the Declaration of Independence was signed, that the Red Sox finally won a World Series, or that a house once burned down in a neighborhood and everyone still remembers it. These places provide the narrative glue for a community, a shared touchstone to history and space. *The Legend of Zelda* did this early in video game history as well, providing enough structure that people could talk about the world, ask one another for advice, and smile knowingly when someone got stuck with a particular puzzle. Miyamoto planned for this, designing a game for which one of his objectives was that people would talk to one another about it. Thus, communities could form around imagined places, building mythologies and narratives that have lasted for the previous thirty years.

Feeling the worlds in the 64 era: Designing for sensory immersion

The next major evolution in these spatial narrative games came with the release of the Nintendo 64 in 1996, which moved Nintendo from 2D to 3D environments. With its release, Miyamoto created *Super Mario 64*

(Nintendo 1996), still the best-selling game on that system (selling 11.89m units [VG Chartz, "Super Mario 64" 2014]), and then two years later (and two years late), Miyamoto released *The Legend of Zelda: Ocarina of Time* (1998). This three-dimensional Zelda still appears on top-rated games lists, and in a retrospective, *Edge* (2014) declares "*Ocarina* may no longer be the prettiest, or even the biggest, but it's still the best of them all." Both of these games continue to organize the narratives within space, but the difference is that the space is modified and has a depth of view that allows for a different type of interaction. Furthermore, these interactions are enabled through the use of a newly designed controller: "*Ocarina* is also a model of how to design for a machine, rather than on it" (*Edge*). Thus, even though these games were designed almost twenty years ago, they defined the conventions for designing in 3D environments.

It often gets said that Miyamoto designed the Nintendo 64 controller for the *Super Mario 64* game, and for people playing *Super Mario 64*, this feels like it could have been the case. The yellow buttons in the right of Figure 2.4 allow the player to change the camera angle. The analog

Figure 2.4 Nintendo 64 controller.
(Photo credit: Judd Ruggill, courtesy of the Learning Games Initiative Research Archive)

stick is pressure sensitive, which means that Mario would tiptoe, walk, and run depending on the pressure.

Further, users could configure the entire controller: They could switch what the buttons do (customizing hardware), or they could hold the controller traditionally, sideways, or upside down (customizing use). However, as Merrick (2000) explains, Miyamoto did not design the controller for only one game: "Mr. Miyamoto wanted analog control because he had a vision of how he wanted that game to work, but the controller wasn't designed specifically for one game." Rather, Miyamoto designed the controller because he had a vision of how the analog stick and the three-dimensional controls would affect different possibilities in gameplay.

What is important to note about *Super Mario 64* is that it's fun. It retains a lot of elements from previous Mario titles and adds the challenge of air travel from *Super Mario Bros. 3* (Nintendo 1988) and *Kirby's Adventure* (Nintendo 1993). However, a large part of what makes this game fun is camera angles, which offer a new way to see the world. In *Super Mario: How Nintendo Conquered America*, Jeff Ryan (2011) notes that Miyamoto had already experimented with 3D in *Super Mario RPG* (Nintendo 1996). However, *Super Mario RPG* used an isometric camera that represented three-dimensional objects in two-dimensional space, and the N64 promised a controllable camera (a promise made real with a controller redesign). However, Miyamoto has said that he returns to games when new possibilities are afforded in the hardware, allowing for new gameplay design options ("Nintendo Power Source" 2000). Thus, Miyamoto didn't want to return to his game *Star Fox* (Nintendo 1993) until emerging technologies would afford different design options. While this seems like a digression here, the fact is that *Star Fox* is the franchise around which Miyamoto started to need 3D space to complete new designs. Then, while working with *Star Fox*, Miyamoto had the idea for a Mario 3D game: "I had always wanted to do a game that recreated an entire world in miniature, like miniature trains" ("The Game Guys" 1996, 24). Interestingly, this idea of miniatures permeates how Miyamoto thinks of design during this era.

When speaking of *The Legend of Zelda: Ocarina of Time* three years later, Miyamoto said, "Instead of thinking of it as making a game, think of it as nurturing a miniature garden called Hyrule" ("Interview: Nintendo Online Magazine" 1998). Returning to Mario though, Miyamoto was under considerable pressure to complete the game; it was a launch title for the new console. However, he continued to feel that it wasn't good enough, pushing off release from 1995 to 1996.

The challenge facing Miyamoto and his team was translating the 2D side-scrolling game into a 3D environment. The enemies still occupied the space and Mario still had to run and jump and collect things, only now he could do so on a Z-axis. "The most difficult part was to realize a virtual 3D world," Miyamoto explained. "It's difficult to give the best 3D angle so that the players don't experience frustration. The game must remain fun to play" (Mielke 1998). To address this problem, Miyamoto turned to cinema. Miyamoto has been very careful to explain that he doesn't create cinema on the game console. He sees cinema as passive whereas games are active. However, he has explained that game designers can borrow good ideas from movies, such as camera angles and real-time voices ("Mr. Miyamoto on Star Fox" 1997, 118), and he sees *Star Fox 64* (Nintendo 1997) as an example of what an interactive movie might be. He explained, "Since I have been working on 3-D games, I have begun to specify camera angles, locations and movement" (Nintendo 1997). And he deftly manages this in his *Super Mario 64* by offering two types of camera control: automatic control to provide "a recommended view" (sometimes the game takes control and offers this when approaching enemies or challenges) and player control, enabling everyone to be "cinematographers."

In addition to this, Miyamoto designed a film crew into the game in the form of the Lakitu Bros. Previous to this game, these cloud-riding characters have thrown spiked turtles at Mario and Luigi, but in this game, the Lakitu Bros. follow Mario around, recording the progress of the main character (see Figure 2.5).

The Lakitu Bros. do not have a long life as cameramen in the Mario-verse (they appear only in two other games: as *Mario & Luigi: Partners*

Figure 2.5 Two screenshots showing a Lakitu cameraman in *Super Mario 64* (one close up and one as a small icon at the bottom right corner of screen).

in Time [Nintendo 2005] and *Paper Mario: The Thousand-Year Door* [Nintendo 2004]), and they do not necessarily influence the trajectory of video games (there is no camera crew following Carl Johnson around in *Grand Theft Auto: San Andreas* [Rockstar Games 2004], for example). What this characterization of a film crews does, however, is provide the player with a useful metaphor to understand camera views in the video game environment. With the launch of the Nintendo 64 and the introduction of a complex controller, Miyamoto and his team at Nintendo had to accomplish two things: (1) teach the player how to navigate this space in order to have a fun and immersive play experience, and (2) teach new developers what is possible with the Nintendo 64 platform. While no other game succeeded in utilizing the Nintendo 64 controller to the same capacity as *Super Mario 64*, this launch title did shape how an emerging 3D video game market would evolve.

In terms of the actual gameplay of *Super Mario 64*, Miyamoto continued to build on the success of the Mario franchise while pulling from his design strategies in *The Legend of Zelda*. According to Ryan, "*Super Mario 64* [is] one of the first sandbox-style games, where there is no time limit or oppressive enemy, but a series of optional side quests. Do them, or just play around in a virtual world" (181). The narrative is still here, driving the objectives of the game. Bowser takes over the castle and imprisons Princess Peach. Mario knows about this only because he is responding to an invitation from the Princess: Peach has made a cake for him. Mario must enter a series of worlds through paintings to collect the stars, eventually releasing Peach from her imprisonment in a stained glass window. She ultimately makes that cake for him. Where the legacy of Zelda can be seen is in the switch from linearity to exploratory behaviors. Mario needs to go through a world and explore the environment. He has to collect all seven stars, and in order to do so, he has to do certain tasks in a certain order. Unlike earlier Zelda games, however, Mario can return and just play in the different environments. It is in *Mario 64* that Miyamoto more fully realizes his design goal of a playground, providing terrain for players to jump, double jump, run, sneak, and fly. The narrative is loose at best, and here, we can see the beginning of a shift to Miyamoto's experience games—games that abandon narratives for simulation, for gameplay, and for communal fun. But before this shift occurs, Miyamoto releases, to great acclaim, *The Legend of Zelda: Ocarina of Time*.

Once again, Miyamoto started designing the Mario and Zelda titles simultaneously. However, *Ocarina of Time* debuted a full two years after *Super Mario 64*. Here, Miyamoto's ambition to have people "feel" a game were realized, at least for him, for the first time. Miyamoto explained during development, "I'm working fulltime on Zelda 64 now. Zelda will be a more realistic emotion adventure than Super Mario 64. I want players to be able to feel the game. They should be able to feel light and shadow, and even temperature and humidity" ("Mr. Miyamoto on Star Fox" 1997, 118). This is an interesting turn for Miyamoto, who has historically focused on what players can *do* in interactive media. With the advent of 3D console technologies, Miyamoto turned his attention and his emotional investment to world building. This is not to suggest that he didn't world build in the past; previous Zelda games were all about exploration. What I mean here is that he wanted an ontological experience between his players and the games, a feeling of being in the world and going somewhere. In Miyamoto's words, "I want them to feel as if they are visiting a place called Hyrule" (Mielke). To help build this experience, Miyamoto and his team ensured that there was a passing of time, with a rising and setting sun, with peaceful fields, and with real-time interactions that are conveyed through cinematic displays. The designers tried to make the objects in the game look like they really existed, using German castles, for example, as reference art.

Time played a role in the narrative as well, with Link moving between his younger self and his older, wiser self. This shift works well to ensure that the game appeals to both newer and younger audiences while also providing older or more experienced players a challenging world to play in. The Nintendo 64 controller, designed to close the gap of immersion, helped the player to navigate in this world. Further, the decision to start the game in Link's childhood increases the connection between the player and avatar. A child Link will need to learn everything from scratch, whereas an adult avatar should already have the skills necessary to sidestep many of the problems. However, in offering time travel, Miyamoto and his designers offer the player a two-part play experience—one in which the player must learn and is innocent, and one in which the player has skills that can save the world. This two-part play experience will set the stage for the darker turn that the Zelda series has in *The Legend of Zelda: Twilight Princess* (Nintendo 2006), but in terms of influence on the game industry, we see here the innate understanding of players and avatars needing to learn material together without lowering the perceived intelligence or the ability of the avatar.

In addition to these narrative uses of time, Miyamoto was interested in using the Nintendo 64 to increase the emotional attachment that players feel with the characters in the game. Miyamoto explains, "Before, in earlier games, we couldn't show the entire game world in detail and we couldn't convey all the emotions of the characters. Now, we can do that on the Nintendo 64. I've always wanted to create realistic experiences, full experiences such as you or I could have, but in exciting worlds" ("The Game Guys," 25). Here, Miyamoto's background in manga can be seen. Miyamoto wanted to create characters with whom we could empathize and sympathize, and in order to achieve this, audiences needed to be able to see the character's emotions on their faces. While he is speaking of *The Legend of Zelda: Wind Waker* (Nintendo 2003) in this following quotation, the same observation can be made about *Ocarina of Time*: "We wanted to make the graphics clearer and because of that, we could show Link's facial expressions. The way Link reacts creates a closer relationship with the player" ("Super Play Magazine Interviews"). The art style is Japanese in that the features are more exaggerated—large eyes to convey emotion, simplified nose and mouth to allow the eyes and body language to do the work of nonverbal communication (see Figure 2.6).

Also of importance in creating *The Legend of Zelda: Ocarina of Time* narrative is the role of the camera. Miyamoto figured out how to manipulate the camera in *Super Mario 64*, testing the camera angles that would be most effective in a video game's 3D environment. In Zelda, the camera becomes something more, a character that speaks to the tensions and emotions throughout the gameplay experience, heightening what the player can feel. Miyamoto spoke to this eloquently in responding to a cinematic question: "With filmmaking, you take several different scenes and later edit them so you can view them as one sequence. In Zelda, things are happening in real time as the camera changes angles and shots. This game is not like a movie, but rather, the camera is becoming the stage performer" ("Interview: Nintendo

Figure 2.6 Screenshot of *The Legend of Zelda: Ocarina of Time*.

Power" 1998). In other words, the camera is a continuous source of input. It is not edited every 2–5 seconds to switch focus. Rather, the camera's focus is always on the protagonist, which is a difficult change to make when adapting movie and cinematic camera techniques to video game spaces. The animators and designers cannot anticipate the angles that the camera may take in following a character or the exact placement in different location to provide, always, the best complement to the emotions and actions of the scene. In this, again, Miyamoto's influence can be seen in the developing three-dimensional narratives that video games will explore in the late 1990s to the present, and it's a trajectory that sees its roots clearly in the dual development of *Mario* and *Zelda* on the Nintendo 64.

Conclusion

In a chapter like this one, it is difficult not to give a careful treatment of each game presented. There is so much more to say about both Mario and Zelda games, such as the masterful use of music, which harkens to Miyamoto's love of listening to and making music himself, to the balance of the games for various demographics. And the topic of music and sound deserves careful consideration as the sounds and soundtracks from Mario, Zelda, and Donkey Kong are part of our idiomatic daily experiences. In addition to how the soundscape affects game play, the fact is that we can indicate (comedic) failure with a three-note desending "wa wa wa" or hum the opening soundtrack from *Super Mario Bros.* to indicate energy. These observations have also influenced video game design and video game culture since the original releases of each game. Also of note as I conclude this chapter is the fact that I underexplore the role of fans. From the release of the first Mario and Zelda games, fans have written into the magazines, professing their love, writing fan fiction in which they are transported to Hyrule, and even sharing fan art and photos of their Mario and Link Halloween costumes.

What these early games give us, I argue, is a trajectory that helps to transition Miyamoto from an aspiring manga artist to a game designer whose main interest is gameplay and connectivity. By this, I mean that his original reliance on narrative to provide objectives and motivations, as well as a framework for the actions, relied on adapting conventions from manga. This can be seen from his early adaptation of the Popeye narrative (Popeye would be called manga in Japan) to his later work that compels the hero through, arguably, the same simplified call to action: A bad guy has the lady; go save her. I do not intend to dismiss the importance of narrative in these games. They set a trajectory for game design that marries other forms of storytelling into an interactive environment. And people love them. What I hope that I have emphasized in this chapter, however, is the ways in which Miyamoto has taken what has historically been linear—narrative structure—and adapted it to the spatial narratives of game space. Furthermore, in adapting these narratives, Miyamoto is not simply telling stories (indeed, he tells interviewers often that he leaves storytelling to the writers); he is providing spaces where I can play a game, allowing the story to unfold on the basis of my action, and allowing me to interpolate myself into imaginary worlds. *I* get to play in the caves of Sonobe; *I* get to return to the playgrounds of my youth.

3

From Games to Experiences: Designing for User Freedom and Unique Expression

One of the challenges in writing about Miyamoto the designer is the nebulous yet ubiquitous influence that he has had at Nintendo since the company's early forays into video games. One year after *The Legend of Zelda: Ocarina of Time* (Nintendo 1998) was released, Miyamoto's *Mario Artist: Paint Studio* (Nintendo 1999) hit the shelves, bundled with the Nintendo mouse. This was the time that Nintendo was attempting to combine home computers with game consoles, a failed bid on their part (Ryan 2011). After this late 1990s' release, Miyamoto had few design or director credits until the release of the Wii and with it *Super Mario Galaxy* (Nintendo 2007). His role largely switched to that of a producer in Nintendo, overseeing the development of consoles and in-house game development while mentoring up the next set of Nintendo designers.

Much can be said about Miyamoto's role as a producer and its effect on the game industry as a whole. For example, Miyamoto produced Tajiri's game *Pokémon: Red and Green* (Nintendo 1996; *Red and Blue* in the United States), which proved to be a resounding success, so much so that the Pokémon Company is the only spinoff subsidiary company in Nintendo. Miyamoto also worked closely with Kojima to translate *Metal Gear Solid* (Konami 2004) to the GameCube, bringing his intimate knowledge of hardware capabilities to bear on the design process of the new Metal Gear title. However, this period is also fraught with lagging GameCube sales, which Miyamoto tried to boost through a series of interviews. Unfortunately, the GameCube had steep competition, with the PlayStation 2 released the year prior in 2000 and the Xbox entering the console market in 2001. Further, the marketing around the Xbox and PS2 created a dichotomy between these sleek, new systems and Nintendo: Nintendo was for children and these new systems were for the hard-core gamer ("Interview: Shigeru Miyamoto and Satoru Iwata" 2002). When asked directly whether Nintendo caters to the casual rather than the hard-core gamer, Miyamoto responded: "At E3 [a gaming trade show], I was a little concerned about defining people as a hard-core gamer vs. a casual gamer. But there are hard-core gamers who play a lot of casual games. Nintendo's focus is to break down the barriers between those two groups and consider everyone just gamers" (Sayre 2007). This trajectory of Miyamoto's game design suggests that he sees gameplay and simulation as the means to break down this barrier, offering people packaged experiences: the experience of owning a dog, of driving in a kart race, of gardening, or of playing baseball.

Miyamoto is not necessarily unique in focusing on experience design. In fact, this is what many game designers do: They turn experiences into systems. The act of play turns those systems back into experiences. A good game designer will be able to anticipate the structural needs for certain experiences and deliver a "good" game to the player. According to Salen and Zimmerman (2004), "Creating great game experiences for players—creating meaningful experiences for players—requires understanding how a game's formal system transforms into an experiential one" (316). For most people who design games, this definition of systematized experience tends to focus on the algorithms, the core mechanics. For Miyamoto, however, game systems need to account for the hardware as well: "The hardware really is the system as a whole" ("Shigeru Miyamoto Roundtable" 2001). Hardware determines the capabilities of the system, such as processor speed and graphics ("Shigeru Miyamoto Roundtable" 2001). In many ways, then, Miyamoto was able to switch his attention to experience design and simulations precisely because of the specific affordances of hardware, and this trajectory brings Miyamoto to the Nintendo DS and Wii, two consoles that outsold competitors (see Figure 3.1).

Such sales figures suggest that Miyamoto's goal to provide everyone a play experience may be, on some level, achievable. I do not claim

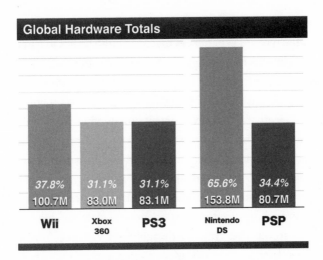

Figure 3.1 Comparative console sale figures.
(Numbers compiled from D'Angelo 2014)

here that Nintendo crushed its competition; the previous and new generation of game consoles, which includes PlayStation and Xbox, proves that this is not another Nintendo versus Sega battle in which one competitor is pushed out of a small pond. Rather, Nintendo's sales numbers support Miyamoto's assertion that "power isn't everything for a console. Too many powerful consoles can't coexist. It's like having only ferocious dinosaurs. They might fight and hasten their own extinction" (Hall 2006). Rather, the Nintendo DS and then Wii provided players with an interface for a different type of game that conveyed a different type of experience. Instead of using the console to fend off aliens and zombies (although you can do that too), players could bowl, catch rabbits, and do yoga. Preceding the Wii's release, however, is an era in which Miyamoto is producing a number of games, and within these games, we can see his shifting emphasis in experience-based games.

This chapter, then, explores Miyamoto's experience-based games. This exploration starts early with the Mario Kart franchise, considers his art-based games, such as *Mario Artist* and *Wii Music* (Nintendo 2008), both of which lay the foundation for his simulation games such as

Pikmin (Nintendo 2001) and *Nintendogs* (Nintendo 2005). In this, I will consider the types of experiences that Miyamoto brings to game design and his evolution from manga-esque storyteller to simulation builder. Throughout his design career, Miyamoto's work has grown to include experiments in experience design that are defined by their emphasis on player creativity and involvement. In moving in this direction, Miyamoto deemphasizes objectives and stories and instead offers frameworks in which players can play around in game communities. To begin this discussion on experience, I turn to Miyamoto's views on violence in games because much of his design energies have been spent on providing alternative experiences to violent video games and alternative stories that typically deemphasize violence. This is not to say that violence isn't in Miyamoto games; rather, the experience of violence, like most other topics, is stylized and informed by his Japanese cultural background and his ultimate goal: to provide everyone a fun-filled and engaging play experience.

Super Smash Bros.: On violence and addiction

It is impossible to talk of a game auteur without a head-nod to the dominant discourses concerning the negative psychological forces of games. As Ken McAllister (2004) notes in his book *Game Work: Language, Power, and Computer Game Culture*, "Almost since their creation, computer games have been both condemned and celebrated for their ability to surreptitiously alter the people who play them" (14). McAllister examines the contradiction in game discourse, noting that within that discourse, computer games are seen as violent, and that violence exerts a force over game players, possibly making them violent. Simultaneously, he notes, computer games teach, and therefore they can be used for educational purposes (McAllister, 15–17). What is interesting about Miyamoto is that he consciously sidesteps these psychological claims, and therefore, his games, which succeed economically and are part of the public discourse, are also largely absent in the debates concerning psychological effect. When asked if he might produce educational games, Miyamoto responded, "No, I don't think my games are effective as education. I think they're more effective in broadening and expanding and bring to life a world for children" ("Shigeru Miyamoto Roundtable" 2001). In other words, educational games are not about fun. And for Miyamoto, games should be about fun, about playing on a playground and playing with others for the sake of playing. Miyamoto's design energies go into creating these play-based lifeworlds, as discussed in Chapter 2.

I bring up educational games because it helps to make sense of his position on violence in video games as well. Violence and negative emotions such as anger and crying are easy experiences and emotions to convey in video games, according to Miyamoto (Palmer 2004). This is not to suggest that Miyamoto shies away from violence in his games. As he said, "It's OK to use violence with quality and for a purpose, but I want to avoid using violence as an easy means just to seek stimulus. We don't have to use it if we have other creative means of expression" ("Interview: Time Digital" 1999). Violence tends not to play a central role in the core gameplay experience of Miyamoto games, although it is almost always there. Mario must smash mushrooms and fire at carnivorous plants; *Zelda*'s entire quest hinges on the player's ability to fight while solving puzzles; and even Donkey Kong pummels the characters on the screen as they try to defeat one another. However, the practice of violence is not the core mechanic; it is a secondary mechanic that allows the drama to rise by heightening tensions. The exception to this is Miyamoto's involvement in the *Smash Bros.*'s franchise.

Super Smash Bros. brings together many of the characters from the Nintendo universe, such as Mario, Kirby, Link, and Pikachu, and puts them into a fighting arena to let the characters battle it out (see Figure 3.2).

The first *Super Smash Bros.*'s game (Nintendo 1999) was given a low budget and little promotion, and Nintendo intended to give it only a limited release in Japan. However, following its success, Nintendo released it to the global market and launched a new line of games

Figure 3.2 Screenshot of *Super Smash Bros.* with four Nintendo universe characters.

based on it, and games in the series went on to win player choice and editorial awards.

The Smash Bros. series is made possible because the Nintendo universe relies on both in-house and second- and third-party development, which means that the characters portrayed in the game have a long history synonymous with Nintendo. And it's fun to play. People can pick any recognizable character from a lineup of protagonists and antagonists. Thus, the series invokes a deep structure to the game precisely because the characters are adapted, intertextually linking to previous games and gameplay experiences. Further, as Hutcheon (2006) has discussed in her book *A Theory of Adaptation*, audience members have a joy, a thrill, when they see something that they loved in one form appear in another form. So while the game would probably be fun with other characters developed specifically for this game, it would probably not be the great success it is because then it would lose the deep structure of the game. Link wouldn't have the Triforce, and Samus wouldn't have her recognizable firearms. Such items create a sense of being in the in-crowd, of knowing what these items are, and what they represent in the original games. Even the option to play the antagonists works similarly; players are as familiar with Bowser and Wario as they are with Mario and Luigi. Further, these antagonist characters are funny in the game, harkening back to Miyamoto's early design decisions around *Donkey Kong*, making the antagonist a funny ape that isn't really all that scary.

While this adaptation speaks to the use of the characters to build brand loyalty to Nintendo, the actual gameplay is indicative of Miyamoto's philosophies on game design. In a 1998 interview, Miyamoto discussed the development of a *Smash Bros.*'s title, explaining, "It may sound like a bloody game if you label it as a fighting game. It's not bloody at all. Instead, it's an enjoyable 'hitting' game like sumo in Japan, in which you have to force your opponent out of a ring, or cage in this case" ("Interview: The 64 Dream" 1998). Oftentimes, it is difficult to pinpoint the cultural influences on Miyamoto's work because so much of his work seems to transcend his Japanese context and perform well in the international market. However, exactly here we can see the influence of a Japanese sport in the ways in which he conceives and then speaks about the *Smash Bros.*'s line. Sumo, for those who have not seen it before, is a ritualistic sport closely linked to Shinto and Shinto's adherence to purification. Sumo wrestlers must purify themselves, throwing salt for this purpose, and only when they feel spiritually ready do they try to knock their opponent from a small ring, often by using flat-handed slaps on the other person.

Sumo is not a violent sport even though the noise is quite shocking when one sits near the ring. Few sumo wrestlers get hurt during a match. But it is a compelling sport to watch. Thus, if Miyamoto is using sumo as his reference to talk about violence, what he is referencing is ritualized competition. Furthermore, we know that Miyamoto, in his role as a producer, affects the central concepts and gameplay of games under his purview, so while he doesn't have design credit here, we can be sure that he has strongly influenced and shaped one of Nintendo's top-selling fighting games—a fighting game that has never been attacked in public opinion. Thus, even when designing a violent video game, Miyamoto does not envision the core experience as violence, and he appears to have pulled off a reinterpretation of the experience of fighting. Instead, he provides people with characters that are recognizable and beloved and gives them a forum for competition. There is no hatred in the game, no egregious baiting. Instead, what players are left with is a sense of good, clean fun. Similarly, in the same way that he retooled the fighting game—a staple for game developers—for new experiences, he successfully redefined the experiences of the racing game with the development of *Super Mario Kart* (Nintendo 1992).

Super Mario Kart: Face-to-face fun

Racing games have always been a mainstay in the video game market, with *Speed Race* (the first racing game, Taito 1974) and *Pole Position* (Namco/Atari 1982) offering players an arcade experience that challenged them to marry timing and time together. As racing games were iterated on, designers punished players for crashing by decreasing fuel (*MotoRace USA*; Irem, 1982) or provided players the added challenge of getting more fuel at predetermined checkpoints (*RoadBlasters*; Atari, 1987). Racing games are well suited to the arcade, providing players a speed-based play experience that seems to rely almost wholly on their skills. In other words, if I go fast enough, I will pass the finish line and be able to continue to the next level. If I do not place high enough in the rankings, then I will need to feed another quarter to continue, but that's okay because it simply means that I wasn't good enough. Further, racing games are short in duration when compared with other arcade games like *Pac-Man* (Namco 1980) or *Donkey Kong* (Nintendo 1981). The controls are simple and recognizable for a driving population—a simple wheel and maybe even a gas pedal and shift stick. Iterative design in racing games focused on adding more realism, better graphics, and different controller inputs. It seemed that this market was defined. Then along came *Super Mario Kart*.

Super Mario Kart is a fast-paced racing game that mimics go-carts rather than racing cars. The carts are humorously subject to the whims of extreme physics, providing the player a racing experience more akin to a Warner Bros.'s cartoon than a Grand Prix simulation. Mario Kart games are always in the top ten best-selling games of any Nintendo system since the franchise first debuted, and often, a Mario Kart game is in the top five best-selling game on the console according to sales numbers on VGChartz (VGChartz, "Super Nintendo Entertainment System" 2014). Further, *Mario Kart* entered the *Guinness Book of World Records* as the most influential video game ever (Ivan 2009). While there is a single-player mode in *Mario Kart*, it is the multiplayer mode that makes this game the extreme success that it is, and it is the multiplayer that allows the team to design in the wacky fun, the quick pace, and the challenge that makes this game a consistent hit across the Nintendo consoles. *Mario Kart's* multiplayer mode entered the public vernacular so much so that people speak of the game with little to no context. Consider this comic from popular web comic XKCD (Figure 3.3):

Figure 3.3 XKCD comic about *Mario Kart* (Monroe 2007).

In the overlay text, this message pops up: "You can evade blue shells in Double Dash, but it is deep magic." The humor of this works by connecting to other's experiences playing this game, and the sales figures suggest that Randal Munroe, XKCD's creator, can safely assume that enough people have played to make this comic viable.

Miyamoto oversaw the production of the game while Tadashi Sugiyama and Hideki Konno directed it. The original plan was to create a game in which two people could play simultaneously (Jones 2011). In an Iwata Asks interview with Miyamoto and Konno, Konno explains that the team decided to use Mario characters only three to four months after game development began; however, the original character placeholder for the game was a guy in overalls ("It Started with a Guy in Overalls" n.d.). The original game offered five modes. The two single-player modes—GP for Grand Prix and Time Trial—were rewarded in typical ways with cups and positions. Then the game offered three two-player modes with a split screen: A Grand Prix (GP), Match Race, and Battle Mode. The Battle Mode offered the players a different way to compete that was not just about ranking. Instead, players had to protect the three balloons surrounding their karts while trying to pop the other person's balloons. And to help the player, the designers brought in slippery banana peels that can be dropped on the racecourse, power-ups, and Koopa shell weapons that can be thrown onto the racecourse, causing havoc for everyone (see Figure 3.4).

Super Mario Kart is fun and funny, but it succeeds at this only because of its multiplayer mode. As Konno explains in a Nintendo Power interview, "When Mario Kart was first developed, our focus was on how the player can have fun and have fun playing with other people" ("Hideki Konno" 2005, 37). We can see here the influence of Miyamoto and his insistence that games should promote people playing together and communicating with one another (a topic that I explore in more depth in the following chapter). What is important to note here is that the emphasis in *Mario Kart* has little to do with the narrative. I write little instead of nothing because *Mario Kart* borrows from the narrative of other Mario games to establish who the good and bad characters are.

Figure 3.4 Screenshot of *Super Mario Kart*; Princess Peach has just thrown a Koopa shell.

The emphasis has to do with designing a game around the emotions of the player, the intention of designing a game around excitement and communication rather than limiting objectives to only winning and speed. Pelland probably captures the feeling of the game best in his Nintendo Power article "The Kart Connection":

> If you've ever felt the thrill of launching a Koopa shell from the back of the pack to decimate an unsuspecting karter on the road ahead, you know what makes the Mario Kart franchise so special. It's all about the interplay of emotions between drivers: like the madcap courses themselves, every race is filled with emotional ups, downs, twists, turns and dozens of small victories and defeats. Though the AI of the Kart games is really very good, the emotional roller-coaster ride is made possible by the unpredictability of human opponents. (2005, 37)

It was this understanding among human opponents that makes the game so fun that drove later developments in *Mario Kart 64* (Nintendo 1996). As Iwata explains, "When the Nintendo 64 came out, Miyamoto-san said that even though the gaming world was heading towards online gaming, we should make games that could be played face-to-face with four of your friends before those days came, and the first four-player game, *Mario Kart 64*, was released" ("It Started with a Guy in Overalls"). With more player inputs, the game became more fun and the antics became more ludicrous. The genius of this game, furthermore, has to do with the fact that any type of player can pick up the game and start to have fun—the entrance points for this franchise is multiaged and multiskilled.

Super Mario Kart has many of the same hallmarks as earlier Miyamoto games. The basic controls are simple, and the basic premise is easy to understand. A player gets a kart. He can control direction and hit buttons to release Koopa shells and other weapons. The courses provide plenty of warning about what's coming so that the player knows when to turn and when to go straight. Thus, even a five-year-old can pick up this game and play it. However, also like earlier Miyamoto games, strategy and tactics can differentiate the play experience, providing a sense of master versus novice. As such, magazines often provided Karting advice to teach people strategies to better their game. For example, *Nintendo Magazine System* offers a "six-page extravaganza," which provides tips and strategies for *Super Mario Kart* ("Super Mario Kart" 1993, 40). Even YouTube has a number of videos that offer strategies and tips for different Mario Kart games. Indeed, the ways in which *Mario Kart* gets discussed has less to do with achieving an end, an objective, and more to do with gaining skills and artistry within a game. *Mario Kart* becomes more like a sport game and less like a narrative-driven game.

It is in *Mario Kart* that we can see the slow evolution of Miyamoto's design goal being achieved. Miyamoto has, from early in his career, discussed the ways in which he wants to create a scaffold for people to do surprising and interesting things, and his personal goal is to surprise them in turn. In responding to what he wants children to learn from his games, Miyamoto said, "I'd like someday to make something in which the players develop their own ideas and vision. Rather than reward them for a single, correct answer, our games encourage them to think of alternatives that lead to different results. I want players to become creative and actively involved" ("Interview: Time Digital" 1999). Miyamoto has found a number of ways to allow for player input and choice to shape the game within the confines of fairly limited affordances. Within the structures of the game, people can develop different styles and goals. Further, Miyamoto's continued involvement with Mario Kart ensured continuity of vision so that, by the time that the Wii was released, Miyamoto worked to create the Wii Wheel, a steering wheel that the Wii Remote could attach to and heighten the challenge of the game. Such evolutions speak to his understanding that hardware is as integral to a game experience as the software.

Mario Paint and *Wii Music*: Player creativity and artistic expression

The same year that *Super Mario Kart* was released, Nintendo also released *Mario Paint* (1992), which Miyamoto produced. Then, for the failed Nintendo 64DD, Miyamoto produced and directed *Mario Artist: Paint Studio* (1999). Miyamoto freely admitted that these programs would probably not be seen as games (IGN Staff 1997); however, the Mario Paint series has close ties to video games because it provides a different way for Nintendo fans to participate in video game culture as creators. Indeed, when asked about their design process for *WarioWare DIY* (Nintendo 2009), the designers tell President Iwata during an Iwata Asks interview that *Mario Paint* was the program that made them interested in making games. Sugioka explains, "When I asked staff members around me about this, a lot of them said that *Mario Paint* was the game that taught them the joy of making games. Especially people in their early twenties" ("A Life-Changing Game" n.d.). Such a quotation suggests that, while the game itself did not change how people designed games, *Mario Artist* brought talent to the game industry that may have otherwise done something else. So while there were minigames in the original *Mario Paint*, the main purpose of the program was to allow people to create freely in the Nintendo universe.

Mario Paint allowed people to draw, use stamps and make custom stamps, and even create short animations and set those animations to music. However, the contemporary critique of the game had to do with the tension between longevity and pricing (*Mario Paint* cost the same as any other Nintendo game); people did not feel that they were getting good value for something that had short-lived novelty ("Mario Paint" 1993). *Mario Artist: Paint Studio* (1999) offered a broader scope of options for players to do, including importing pictures and film clips. This version also had a series of expansion packs, such as *Talent Studio*, *Polygon Studio*, and the Communication Kit. Further, in keeping with Miyamoto's belief that games should bring people together, *Mario Artist* had a four-person paint option. In these two programs, it appears that Nintendo and Miyamoto are providing people with a simple paint program packaged in Nintendo brands such as Mario. However, the theories behind these titles speak more to the idea of player creation: Miyamoto and others at Nintendo want to provide players the freedom to create artistically, to play around, and to share their works with others. This is also the philosophy that drove Miyamoto and his team in creating *Wii Music* (2007).

While I discuss the majority of Miyamoto's design credits for the Wii in the following chapter, I move my consideration of *Wii Music* here because it has more in common with *Paint Studio* than with *Wii Sports* or *Wii Fit* (Nintendo 2007). Miyamoto both produced and designed for *Wii Music*, creating a game that almost has a jazz underpinning. One could argue that the expression of jazz has much in common with painting—the object is defined, yet the personal expression changes based on the creator. In *Wii Music*, the object of the game is to arrange music by conducting through a band that is on the screen, bringing in musical instruments, and improvising when needed. Its contemporaries, the *Guitar Hero* (Harmonix 2005) and *Rock Band* (Harmonix / Pi Studios 2007) games, also ask players to make music, but the idea in these games is to get a high score and hit all of the notes perfectly. *Wii Music* is not this. According to Miyamoto, "It's something we made with the idea of turning the joy of music into a game. It isn't a musical instrument, but it isn't a video game, either. It's something like no other" ("The Joy of Playing Music" n.d.). Kohler (2008) adds to this, explaining, "The challenge is not to complete the song 'perfectly'—it's to create something that sounds nice by artfully arranging your playing style and choosing complementary instruments. Aside from a few snags in the process, it works." The problem, Kohler identifies, is that *Wii Music* is not a plug-and-play sort of game. With games like *Guitar Hero*, the player knows what he needs to do; the objective is measured with points and feedback. *Wii Music*, on the contrary, is about open creativity, about making the game into a type of musical instrument. Miyamoto explained that he wanted people to have a high degree of expression (Kohler 2008). The challenge was that people didn't understand the game; they needed to pick it up and play with it before it made sense. Moreover, with games costing as much as they do (*Wii Music* sold for $40 new), these are expensive gambles.

These three creative titles did not do well in sales. *Mario Artist: Paint Studio* only had a Japanese release, and according to the following sales numbers on VGChartz, *Mario Paint* (Nintendo 1992) only sold 2.75 million units. *Wii Music* was the weakest of the Wii launch titles, selling only 3.22 million in total worldwide sales. Compare this to *Super Mario Galaxy* (Nintendo 2007) with 11.09 million units, or even *Wii Fit* (Nintendo 2007), which included the purchase of additional hardware, with 22.69 million units. Such sales figures may indicate that these failed titles are outliers in Miyamoto's corpus, but that is not the case. In many ways, these games are creative experiments, instantiations of Miyamoto's interests, and his attempts to translate those interests into gamespace for others to enjoy. Iwata rightly points out in his interview with Miyamoto that Miyamoto's background in music and his philosophies and interests in music inform the creation of a game like *Wii Music* ("Shigeru Miyamoto's Early Encounters with Music" n.d.). Moreover, we know that Miyamoto wanted to be a manga artist and enjoyed the process of drawing and creating visuals. Thus, the Mario Artist games are systematic programs that make tools and techniques available to those who would also like to create.

Furthermore, Miyamoto has long struggled (and often succeeded) in providing players with just the right amount of direction and just the right amount of freedom to allow for player creation and expression (see games like *Super Mario Bros.* and *The Legend of Zelda* for early examples of where he got this right); games like the *Mario Paint* titles and *Wii Music* speak more to the fact that Miyamoto simply provided too much freedom and not enough objectives. It's not that Miyamoto cannot translate his interests, hobbies, and experiences into games successfully, because he did, and to resounding success in such titles as *Pikmin*, *Nintendogs*, and *Wii Fit*, and tangentially in games like *Wii Sports* (2006) and *Animal Crossing* (or *Animal Forest* as it's known in Japan; Nintendo 2002). It's that Miyamoto was trying to translate artistic endeavors into game space, and art is a strange combination of training, intuition, skill, craft, style, and dedication. Sometimes, people just want games, not a program that will take years to master on a game system. And sometimes they just want short, casual games. Miyamoto understood this as well, and this is also the era in which he created a number of casual games based on the ethic of care.

Designing emotional attachment: The beginning of casual games

Miyamoto got his start early in the history of video games, designing games with simple controls and game mechanics. Thus, it comes as little surprise that he was poised to design games for what Jesper Juul (2010) calls the "casual revolution." According to Juul, the casual revolution "is the moment in which the simplicity of early video games is being rediscovered, while new flexible designs are letting video games fit into the lives of players" (2). Video games are for everyone, meeting the needs of a diverse player base of any age. What Juul speaks of as a distinctly contemporary phenomenon is what has guided Miyamoto's design philosophy since his entrance into the gaming industry. Miyamoto has explicitly said, "I want as many people around the world as possible to play my games" ("Interview: GamePro" 2002), and to achieve this, he designs games that have multiple entrance points for varying game skills. In addition, he puts his games through rigorous testing, spending the bulk of his development time on polishing the game based on player feedback.

Miyamoto created the concepts behind and produced both *Pikmin* and *Nintendogs*. Directed by Shigefumi Hino and Masamichi Abe, *Pikmin* is a game about growing and cultivating a symbiotic relationship between Olimar, a space alien who has crashed on a planet, and little Pikmin, small vegetation-based animals that must be planted and harvested. Olimar uses the Pikmin to find the parts of his spaceship, and the Pikmin are raised and kept safe from nighttime dangers by Olimar. The narrative call to action for this game is the need to collect all of the spaceship parts before Olimar's life support runs out. However, in the challenge mode, all the player has to do is to grow as many Pikmin as possible in one day. As can be seen in Figure 3.5, the graphics in *Pikmin* are characteristic of many Nintendo titles: bright primary colors and charming cartoon-like exaggerated features.

The soundtrack complements the game as well, with music that sounds like a comedic stroll through the woods and the happy, cele-bratory voices of the captain and the Pikmin accompanying almost all

Figure 3.5 Screenshot of *Pikmin*.

actions. As Gestalt writes in his 2001 review of the game, "Designed by the legendary Shigeru Miyamoto, at first sight it looks like just another zany kids game with its brightly coloured graphics and cartoonish characters. But dig a little deeper and you find one of the console's most innovative and downright fun games." The innovation comes not from searching and collecting items—Miyamoto has already implemented that into game design—but from the growing and deploying characters that you as the player have responsibility for. It's hard not to smile when playing *Pikmin*.

Nintendogs, too, depends on the player opting into a relationship of care for their electronic pets. Directed by Kiyoshi Mizuki and produced by both Hideki Konno and Shigeru Miyamoto, *Nintendogs* complements the handheld DS system on which it was released in 2005, using its touchscreen and microphone as inputs for gameplay (see Figure 3.6).

The concept is simple: The player has a virtual dog. She can use the microphone to call the dog, talk to the dog, blow bubbles for the dog, and even teach it tricks such as to sit and roll over. In addition to that, the player can use the touch screen to pet the dog and play with it.

Figure 3.6 Screenshot of playing *Nintendogs*.
(Courtesy of Stephanie Vie)

Players can take the dog for walks, buy it toys, and simply watch it as it acts cute on the screen (and the dogs do act cute). Also, because the DS has networking capabilities, players can introduce their dogs to their friend's dogs, and their dogs can play on the same screen in Bark Mode.

These games move away from objective-based games and into the realm of care-based games. There are still objectives in the game and they even include minigames; however, the core game mechanic is about taking care of and nurturing gardens or animals. The player does not need to spend time with strategy guides, disciplining himself to be a better racer, nor does he need to find the hidden dungeon, or even jump on a turtle in a certain way for the promise of infinite lives. Rather, the player logs in and cultivates a garden of tiny, cute Pikmin or takes care of and plays with small, computerized dogs. The player is not punished in the game; there is no guilt associated with neglect. So long as the player remembers to call the Pikmin home at night, they will live until the next player can play. Even if the player ignores the Nintendogs for months, when there is a next chance to play again, the waiting dogs can be baited into a good mood easily with a little simulated care.

These care-based games were not common at the time that Miyamoto was creating the concepts for the games. There was, of course, *Tamagotchi* (Bandai 1996), the small egg-shaped pet on a keychain that needed constant feeding and cleaning up after. Generations 1 and 2 of the *Tamagotchi* game sold well (1.45 million units in global sales [VGChartz]). However, the problem with these early games is that the small electronic pet would die quickly without care—if a child went to school and was not able to tend their Tamagotchi, then they would return home to a dead virtual pet. This meant that children were playing them in the classroom, trying to keep their Tamagotchi alive. Such dedicated care is stressful, and Miyamoto had to have accounted for it while overseeing the production of *Pikmin* and *Nintendogs*. In discussing both *Pikmin* and *Animal Crossing*, Miyamoto explained that he was ruminating on what might compel people to play and enjoy games regardless of their age. What he came up with is "something fun that makes you feel that you're playing a game but not tired, just fun" ("Interview: Famitsu" 2001). This shift in game design decreases the stressful part, the grinding through levels, and allows the player to play.

Pikmin and *Nintendogs* were both new franchises born in the early 2000s. This is significant because Miyamoto launched all the franchises for which he was the lead designer or concept creator in the 1980s with Mario, Zelda, and Donkey Kong. This is not to indicate that Miyamoto avoided creativity at this time; rather, his switch to producer was a role in which he mentored other game designers to think about game design similarly. What is interesting here in terms of game creation, however, is that Miyamoto returned to his roots in game design, falling back on his nongamic hobbies to create games. For example, as I discussed in Chapter 2, Miyamoto's inspiration for *Donkey Kong* came from his background in manga and his love of movies and adapting readily available narratives (such as Popeye). Mario and Zelda drew inspiration from childhood exploration of either playgrounds or the natural surroundings of Sonobe. These two later games, likewise, draw on Miyamoto's interests and hobbies—gardening and dog ownership—interests and hobbies that are more mature and belong to an adult sensibility rather than childhood memories.

In this, Miyamoto enacts his design vision, looking to his world and experiences to provide inspiration for his games. He has talked about his inclination to speak to all kinds of people about different topics that have nothing to do with games, and from these conversations, he finds out what motivates people and brings them joy. Further, he speaks against the habit of game designers to look only to their own industry for creative ideas (Baratto 2002). In a 2002 IGN interview, he explained, "If you look too inwardly [at the gaming industry] it can be hard to approach fun and games from a fresh perspective. It is good to be open to new possibilities exposing yourself to a wide theatre of experiences and find inspiration in unlikely places. For example I like *Pikmin*, which I made after being in my own garden" ("Nintendo Roundtable" 2002). The human experience, in other words, runs broad, yet Miyamoto is right to indicate that most games are iterations of either previous games or of established narrative forms. When game designers shift their focus to the breadth of human experience, then simple activities such as gardening become fodder for algorithms and representation. And they should be. People enjoy and play at any number of activities, and computer games have the capacity to provide an environment for people to experience certain aspects of those activities.

Even in these games, though, there is a sense of continuity in vision. As I discussed in Chapter 2, Miyamoto was interested in designing games that were essentially miniature gardens—players could look down on a complete world and see the actions of the characters. In discussing these early games and their relation to narratives, Dymek (2010) writes,

> Miyamoto's reference to the "exploration" of a "miniature garden" implies a simulational rather than a representational approach—he wants to convey the fascinating feeling of exploring nature by creating a "miniature" that gamers can use on their own, i.e. a video game that simulates the experience of nature exploration. A "narrative" does not drive this simulation, although his memories of childhood might, quite exaggeratedly, be considered "narratives" from his youth that are being transmitted through the game mechanisms. (426)

In these later games, a narrative doesn't drive the simulation; rather, his joy at gardening and owning a dog do. Further, this sense of having a miniature garden is fully realized in something like *Pikmin*, which is literally a miniature garden. The hand of the player manipulates the world, but the actions integral to the game are those of the nonplayer characters, not the player character. The player watches the antics of the garden species (or the dogs), and the joy of play comes from watching the environment and nonplayer characters reacting to simple actions on the part of the player.

Miyamoto develops this idea of manipulating other movements as the central action of gameplay in both the games. *Nintendogs* requires the "owner" of the dog to do certain things, like taking the dog to the gym for training or buying the dog special treats. When players do things for the dog, such as pet or feed their pet, the dog reciprocates with equal caring. One player meets up with another player, and if both people have a DS with *Nintendogs*, then the DS will network the games so that the two players' dogs can interact with one another on one screen—all the player has to do is to sit back and watch the dogs do cute dog things. There is almost no player interaction in this case; the game becomes a spectator sport, much like owning a real dog. In other words, the dogs are always responding to environmental and player stimulation rather than being directed by the player.

This is similar to what happens in *Pikmin*, although in this game, the player can direct the small garden creatures, much like a parent directs children to do certain things. In speaking about the game, Miyamoto explained, "Pikmin do all the work, while you don't do anything directly, but you are busy in giving them instructions. I wanted to make an action game, in which you weren't directly involved" ("Interview: Famitsu" 2001). Such a game fundamentally changes the expectations of games that are ludically defined. By this, I am drawing on Caillois' definitions in *Man, Play, and Games* (1961) and the ways that these theories are adapted by scholars such as Frasca to elucidate a continuum between play and games. In this seminal work, Caillois attempts to delineate between play (paidia) and games (ludus). Paidia, or play, covers "the spontaneous manifestations of the play instinct" (27–28). Play is a free and carefree enacting of fantasy and diversion from everyday life (13). Ludus, on the contrary, "encompass the various games to which, without exaggeration, a civilizing quality can be attributed. In fact, they reflect the moral and intellectual values of a culture as well as contribute to their refinement and development" (27). Ludus, for Caillois, is the ways in which we codify the systems of our world, providing us scaled frameworks to learn and practice within shared rule sets. Frasca (2003) elaborates on Caillois' theories in his attempt to delineate between games and stories. Frasca draws on Andre Lalande's 1928 work *Dictionaire Philosophique* to define paidia as free play that has no objective and is meant for pleasure only, and ludus is a closed rule system that defines the conditions for winning or losing (Frasca 1999; see also Frasca 2003).

In Frasca's 1999 work, there is a strict binary between play and games, and some of this has to do with the fact that Frasca's work comes early in game studies and our attempt to define terms.

Thus, Jensen (2013) is largely correct when he writes that Frasca's definitions "effectively preclude the possibility of movement between the two 'genres' and thus undermines the transformative and generative power of play, which is derived precisely from the point at which *paidia* and *ludus* necessarily intersect" (emphasis in original). Frasca's definitions are a useful way to think about games and play on a continuum (see Figure 3.7). Any game based on player motivation and skill can be located on a ludus-paidia continuum. Figure 3.7 provides an example of this, using the game *Super Mario Bros.* It has clear objectives, requires skills that players must master, and has win-and-lose conditions. Thus, when players subject themselves to those rules and try to win, they are playing the game based on the ludic constraints (get to the end of level 1-1, preferably with the most points). However, Miyamoto designed into the game different ways to interact with the environment, and he has even talked about the ways in which players can play the game differently, such as overlaying "house rules" like avoiding all coins. Or players can treat the game like the playgrounds that inspired *Super Mario Bros.*, messing around, breaking bricks, and

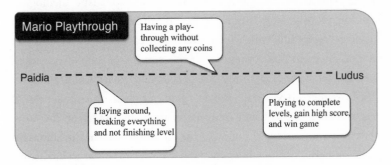

Figure 3.7 A *Super Mario Bros.* playthrough on a paidia/ludus continuum.

doing tricks with turtles, ignoring completely the gamic elements. In other words, players who subject themselves to the rules and objectives of the game are closer to ludus whereas those players who ignore the rules of the game and play around in the space are closer to paidia. Some games, within their rule sets, are more situated on this continuum as more rule-bound (ludus) or more freeplay (paidia). This is the shift that Miyamoto makes in these later experience-based games.

In designing *Pikmin* and *Nintendogs*, Miyamoto conceived of games that support paidia. *Pikmin* does have objectives and a win/lose condition, but the joy of playing the game is in the paidia, in the freeplay. *Nintendogs*, on the contrary, presents the player with no win condition in the main game, and the objectives are tenuous at best: Your dog should be happy. Objectives are included only in the minigames; dogs can win agility trials, for example. The embrace of paidia may constitute a shift from games to simulations; however, this debate doesn't serve an interrogation of Miyamoto's design philosophies because his games have always been simulations of experiences. This shift merely sees the ludic rules move from the objectives of the game to the algorithms of the game. The rules are still there and still define what people can do. Then, when we look to games like *Nintendogs*, the game board—the rules and objectives that dictate success in the game—are care and pet ownership within a capitalist system. As Andy Myers notes in his 2005 review "Man's Best Friend," "Everything costs money in *Nintendogs*, including water" (45). Such an observation of course opens *Nintendogs* up to critiques of capitalistic ideological training, yet Miyamoto is transferring his experience of dog ownership in his everyday life, which is imbricated in capitalist purchasing and care practices. In this, *Nintendogs* joins a number of simulation games, such as *The Sims* (Electronic Arts 2000) and *Roller Coaster Tycoon* (Hasbro Interactive 1999), providing players with the challenges of resource management and rewards. In their discussion of *The Sims*, Nutt and Railton (2003) note that the contradictions in the landmark game adhere to the contradictions of Western late capitalism—instrumentality and friendship, consumption and care, or even play and obligation. The same can be said of *Nintendogs*: Owning a dog in life costs money, and it is the earning and spending of money that adds challenge and objectives to the game. Further, these are the systems in which people play every day, so creating a game from these systems ensures a transferability, a sense of control, and a scale that is sized for individual players to succeed in.

Conclusion

In his book *A Casual Revolution: Reinventing Video Games and Their Players*, Jesper Juul (2010) proposes three nesting frames for understanding video games. At its core, and constant across all games, is the goal orientation or desire to win. Surrounding this is frame two, the game as experience, which represents people's desire for interesting games. The final frame includes these other two and adds to it a social component—people desire social events and want to manage social situations (127). Building up to this framework, Juul discusses *Animal Crossing*, a village simulation game that requires people to collect objects, build houses and then bigger houses, and give gifts in social frameworks. Ian Bogost (2008) takes *Animal Crossing* to task for providing a procedural rhetoric for capitalist models, which include "arguments about how social, cultural, and political processes work" (126). However, what Juul gives us is a different way to understand games like *Animal Crossing* as being games that allow people to play for personal and communal goals, thus making games socially meaningful (126)—in a word: Communication.

Since very early in his design career, Miyamoto has always emphasized communication and community in his games. As I discussed in Chapter 2, *The Legend of Zelda* has, as one of its central design components, communication within groups. Miyamoto wanted people to talk with one another about the game and puzzles. In his 2007 GDC Keynote, Miyamoto explains that Zelda provided the inspiration for *Animal Crossing*, a game that was based almost exclusively on communication ("A Creative Vision"). And this type of game reaches a wider audience. In speaking about *Animal Crossing*, Miyamoto explained, "That's the type of game, where if a hardcore gamer was to pick it up and evaluate it, it probably wouldn't get a very high rating. Things that a hardcore gamer looks at are game balance, game difficulty, the number of bosses, the number of levels and the AI. This game has none of those things. But when you sit down and play this game, it's fun" ("Interview: CVG" 2002). The ease and fun of this game and ones like it appeal to a wide audience, inviting players to play these casual games for hours.

Looking at this production era of game development, Miyamoto's influence continues to have a firm foothold in the game industry. He and his cohort at Nintendo are at the forefront of the casual games movement, translating their previous game design experiences and their real-world experiences into gameplay. Not only can we see the influence of Miyamoto's early work on this generation of games (*Zelda* providing inspiration for *Animal Crossing*, for example), but also we can see the influence of these experience games on contemporary casual games. In a media industry that adheres to the axiom "tried and true with a twist," we see the twists presented by *Farmville* (Zynga 2009) or *Flutter* (Runawayplay 2013) and understand their clear connections to these Nintendo games. Further, this phase in Miyamoto's career saw a shift from designer to mentor—the sheer number of successful games that he produced and the clarity of the core gameplay concepts strongly suggest his continued influence on an emerging generation of game designers. However, it is with the next generation of consoles and the release of the Nintendo Wii that Miyamoto starts to directly touch the game industry through his design once again.

4

Revolutionizing Gameplay: Casual Games and Mature Audiences

In 2006, a series of commercials entitled "Wii for All" followed two Japanese Nintendo representatives as they traveled the United States, hooking up the Wii and letting a diverse segment of the population play the new Nintendo console. The bulk of the commercial was spent watching these people—suburban families bowling, a grandfather with his family moving his body, urban twenty-somethings watching one another, and a couple of rural farmers driving race cars—playing the Wii, acting like fools, and having a gloriously good time together. As Wesley and Barczak (2010) have rightly pointed out, this marketing campaign saw a shift from the technologies of the system to showing players in game (150–51), and to this observation, I would add that these commercials showed players in their groups and communities. Play is a communal act, and the Wii promises to deliver such instances of community. Nintendo and Miyamoto obviously identified a desire in the consumer base, because even though the Wii itself was technologically less sophisticated than its contemporary competition, the Xbox 360 and the PS3, it was the best-selling console of that generation.

The Wii also marks a turning point for Shigeru Miyamoto. After a long period of time as a game producer, Miyamoto turned back to game design with the release of the Nintendo Wii. This new console, in many ways, returns Miyamoto to his roots, and here, we can clearly see the influence of both his industrial design background as well as his years of mentoring at the hand of Gunpei Yokoi. Developed under the codename Revolution, the Wii would catapult Nintendo back into the home, a recognizable brand in front of each television. Nintendo had been struggling in the home console market with the GameCube, yet Nintendo was still in a strong position with DS sales.[1] So for the Wii's release, Miyamoto created concepts and designs for such recognizable titles as *Wii Sports* (Nintendo 2005), *The Legend of Zelda: Twilight Princess* (Nintendo 2006), *Super Mario Galaxy* (Nintendo 2007), *Wii Fit* (Nintendo 2007), and the previously discussed *Wii Music*. Players can swing their swords to play Zelda; they can simulate bowling actions; and they can point to where they want Mario to fly. The inputs of the Wii Remote allow people to have a fundamentally different play experience while still transferring the skills developed on past controllers. This is the mimetic gameplay that Juul (2010) describes in *A Casual Revolution* as being important to ushering in casual games.

In this chapter, I consider this era in Miyamoto's career with a special eye to his dual emphasis on hardware and software/game development. First, I discuss the Wii console and Miyamoto's involvement with the new direction of Nintendo's games. Following this, I turn my attention to Miyamoto's classic games on this new platform, namely, *Super Mario Galaxy* and *The Legend of Zelda: Twilight Princess* to consider the evolution of Miyamoto's designs in these classic franchises and the ways in which they highlight the affordances of the new Wii hardware. Finally, I turn to *Wii Fit* and the expansion of the market to mothers and wives, a metric that Miyamoto uses to gauge his own success. The challenge of this chapter, of course, is that I must rely somewhat on speculation because the influence of these games cannot yet be measured, and his future projects have not yet been released. However, there can be no doubt that the Nintendo Wii and Miyamoto once again disrupted the game industry, showing what is possible when design goals focus on experience and expanding markets.

---

[1] Nintendo has sold 154.88 million units of the DS handheld system, second only to the PlayStation 2, which has sold 157.68 units (VGChartz, "Platform Totals" 2014). However, it's worth noting that the PS2 was available from 2000 to 2013 whereas the DS was only available from 2004 to 2007—one-third of the total market time of Sony's best-selling console.

"Wii Would Like to Play": Creating novel inputs

Novel interfaces for game controls are fairly common in Japanese arcades, which differentiate themselves from the home market by offering players with unique hardware. People who visit arcades in Japan are likely to see traditional Taiko drums, sound boards, motorcycles, dance pads, and complex control boards for a range of games (see Figure 4.1).

The controls for the game matter as much for the play experience as the game itself. Further, these controls offer the player a chance for performativity in public spaces—good players attract spectators, so players are judged by both the algorithms of the game for technical proficiency and by spectators for style and entertainment.

Figure 4.1 *Taiko no Tatsujin* in a Japanese arcade (Namco 2001; *Taiko Drum Master* in the United States).

(Photo credit: Used with permission from traveljapanblog.com: http://traveljapanblog. com/wordpress/2012/06/taiko-no-tatsujin-arcade-game/)

The Wii's revolution was essentially a change in the controller interface, and this change was intended to make gaming a communal activity while also enhancing the connection between the body and play activities on the screen. The Wii console itself, however, is not the most advanced of its generation—indeed, it is essentially a modified GameCube, which was released in 2001, making the Wii's technology essentially five years out of date. Such a decision may have been risky, for as Ruggill and McAllister (2011) have noted, gaming technologies are always anachronistic: They are built on old tropes and technologies for play (both hardware and software) but are trying to anticipate new technologies and types of play for future development. Most game console developers focus their energies on the hardware in the console; Nintendo shifted their attention to the input device of the Wii Controller.

This decision to recycle GameCube technologies has a long precedent at Nintendo, and here too, we can see the influence of Yokoi on Miyamoto's hardware design approaches. Yokoi's philosophy of "lateral thinking with withered technology" approaches hardware design in cost-effective and innovative ways. For example, when Yokoi was developing the Game Boy, he made the argument to use monochromatic screens even though their competitors at Atari and Sega were developing portable gaming devices with color screens. This decision helped to keep the price of the unit down—the Game Boy cost $89.99 at release, while the Atari Lynx was $189.95 and the Sega Game Gear was $149.99—and it prolonged battery life to about 10–12 hours rather than the 4–5 hours of competing handheld units. Thus, while the technology was not the most cutting edge, the play experience was comparable to its competitors, and the older technologies had tangible benefits in terms of cost and playtime, ensuring the Game Boy's success in those early generations of handheld devices.

Similarly, the development team for the Wii, which included Miyamoto, opted to use "withered technology" for new purposes. And like the Game Boy, the price reflected this technological recycling: The Wii launched at $249.99 while the PlayStation 3's launch price was $499, and the Xbox offered two prices, one basic model at $299 and the premium package at $399. Further, this older technology had a development history—the technology did not have a steep learning curve for game developers. Thus, as Wesley and Barczak have noted, "the development cost for a Nintendo game ranged from 25 to 50 percent of the cost of a similar Xbox 360 or PlayStation 3 title. Development cycles were significantly shorter, allowing publishers to produce more games in the same amount of time" (145). This is important for Nintendo, which makes the bulk of its profit from licensing agreements with other developers. Nintendo's in-house development exists to make games that sell the Nintendo consoles (Gaudiosi 2005); this in-house development is a necessary investment to ensure that more consoles end up in the home. Once these consoles are in the home, second- and third-party developers can create games for the system. This benefits Nintendo because these licensees must pay a sales percentage to the Nintendo company for every unit sold.

Further, by choosing to approach the console design differently from Sony and Microsoft, Miyamoto and his colleagues redefined the metrics of success. In his article "Nintendo: Wii Want to Expand Games' Appeal," Kenji Hall (2006) writes, "Miyamoto, a senior managing director, says it's Iwata's way of getting his own people to stop obsessing about power. 'The media likes to refer to this as the "war of next-generation consoles,"' says Miyamoto, the inventor of Mario Bros. and Zelda who now leads hardware platform and game software development. 'But that implies that we have the same strategy as the others.'" Rather than getting into a race where dinosaurs devour one another, Miyamoto and other senior executives decided to switch their hardware design focus from developing more powerful consoles to developing family-friendly consoles that promoted collaborative fun and innovative game design. Their purpose was to get more people playing games that otherwise might not. As Dymek (2010) writes:

> The Wii, and Miyamoto's vision of video gaming, illustrate how there are indeed influential alternatives to the hardcore gamer-based industry spiral of creative conservatism and its limited range

of mono-thematical esoteric subcultural content. Furthermore, by not over-investing in the console technological rat race the Wii has been cheaper in design and production, thus not requiring subsidizing and decreasing significantly Nintendo's risk. In other words, the Wii is successful both in terms of medium/content innovation as well as industrial/production economics. The Wii truly vindicates that alternative industry logic can exist successfully commercially and artistically in today's industry context. (426)

The artistic approach that the Wii provided was an alternative input device for home consoles via new controllers. Within this iterative development, we can see the Japanese situational influence, as well as Miyamoto's long history as an industrial engineer who has a say in controller development, come to the forefront. The base technology of the hardware was not obsolete yet; it just needed to be reimagined with a new input controller for people to design for the system.

Miyamoto prides himself on having a role in the design of every Nintendo game controller since the Famicom or Nintendo Entertainment System. Here, it would be useful to go back to comments that Miyamoto makes regarding his influence on the Nintendo DS, a highly successful handheld system (for more on this, see Tobin 2013). In a 2004 Game Spy interview, Miyamoto explained,

> I would go and look at things like the distance between the two screens, and what would be the best distance in terms of gameplay. I looked at button positioning and things like that and how they would affect the gameplay and how players can play with them. I have an industrial design background; but as hardware designers, they don't like to hear me talk about my background. I try to stick to more gameplay-oriented comments.

Thus, with the DS, what Miyamoto was aiming for was an early arcade experience of "direct control": the jump button jumps, and that's it. The player feels that they are directly controlling the character ("E3 2004").

Miyamoto's industrial design approach, along with his goals for direct control, shapes his input on the Wii Remote. The Wii Remote,

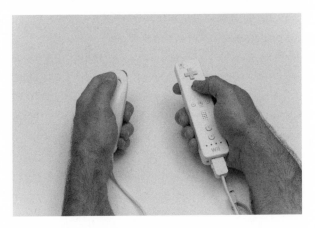

Figure 4.2 Wii Remote and Nunchuk.
(Photo credit: Aaron McGaffey)

or Wiimote as it is sometimes called, can be used in two ways: as a motion-based controller (interfacing with the sensor bar place on top of the television) or as a traditional controller when turned on its side (see Figure 4.2).

Players can wrap the safety strap around their wrists and control the game with their movements, "A" button, and trigger. Sometimes, they are called upon to use the D-pad at the top of the controller. When the Wii Remote is turned on its side, then the controller provides the player a more traditional interface akin to the early NES console with one hand controlling the D-pad and the other using buttons 1 and 2 for additional input. Yet as Jones and Thiruvathukal (2012) note in *Codename Revolution: The Nintendo Wii Platform*, "the Wii Remote alone is inadequate. So Nintendo developed a plan to treat the Wii Remote as a hub for various extension peripherals" (55). The Nunchuk above is the most common of these, packaged with the Wii console and Wii Remote. In addition to this is also the driving wheel or the Wii Fit platform.

All of these redesigns spoke to Miyamoto and Nintendo's desire to expand their market and get people who would not normally play video games to pick up a controller. Miyamoto often speaks of this as a Mom test (Hall 2006) or Wife test (Miyamoto 2007), looking to middle-aged women as a metric for success. In this way, Miyamoto is attempting to expand the market from that "core" gamer—the young male—by specifically targeting an underserved population. It must be noted, however, the problematic approach of defining the demographic thusly: women's identities are subsumed under the categories of "wife" and "mother." Nevertheless, it is with this demographic in mind that Miyamoto turned his attention to the controller. The controller, according to Miyamoto, limited games' accessibility. Miyamoto explained:

> Speaking as the individual who created the traditional controller, I certainly don't want to speak badly of it! I think as videogames evolved, the videogame experience became more complicated. In order to control the more complicated experience, that resulted in more complicated controllers. The challenge of that is that videogames then became something that appeared to be difficult and complicated to people who don't play videogames. So what we've been trying to do over the last few years is find ways to take advantage of technology to essentially create an interface that has a broader appeal and that's more approachable to the average consumer. (Kohler 2008)

Here, we see a return to Miyamoto's philosophy of direct control. As controllers became more complicated, people had to be able to navigate upward of ten input devices to play a game, meaning that the player had to become a controller expert in order to fully play and appreciate the game. This is a high investment of time and training, and as such, it turned many people away who were not interested in gaining the necessary skills. Had Nintendo continued to create consoles with complex controls, they would have been directly competing with Sony and Microsoft for the same type of gamer and would have been providing a platform for the same types of games. Instead, Miyamoto and Nintendo opted for a different market, still related, but simplified and therefore broader. Once the console was released, Miyamoto was called upon to develop games that would show the possibilities of this new interface. Miyamoto became a game designer again.

Mario and Zelda again: Tensions between games for everyone and games for mature audiences

It's hard to think of a Nintendo console without Mario and Zelda titles, and the Wii was no exception. For this effort, Shigeru Miyamoto returned to direct input on games; he was the game concept designer for *Super Mario Galaxy*, the general producer, and one of the writers for *Super Mario Galaxy 2* (Nintendo 2010), and started as director for *The Legend of Zelda: Twilight Princess*. Worth noting here is that the Wii is the first console that is accompanied by a Zelda title at release—*Twilight Princess*—and this concurrence is largely due to the fact that the design team could design for the GameCube and reconfigure the controls for the Wii Remotes. These three games are highly regarded titles in the Wii game library. In fact, both *Twilight Princess* and *Super Mario Galaxy 2* were included in the Smithsonian's "The Art of Video Games" exhibit. What we can see in this generation of Miyamoto's design vision is his continued dedication to designing games that highlight Nintendo hardware and his core design philosophy that gameplay matters above all else. While these games speak to Miyamoto's successes, reception of these games also speak to a playing public that wants more from their play experience, something more mature and gritty—what *Twilight Princess* became under the direction of Eiji Aonuma. Before turning my discussion to the demands of the mature audience, however, I would first like to look to the Super Mario Galaxy games to trace the evolution of gameplay design to its current form.

As I discussed in Chapter 2, early Mario games offered multilayered worlds that were spatially organized both horizontally (side scrolling) and vertically (sky, dungeon, and underwater levels). By using space in these innovative ways, Miyamoto was able to hide secrets and mysteries in familiar landscapes, allowing players to discover new worlds if they explored the maps available. *Super Mario 64* translates this into the 3D environment, offering players a playground-esque experience through Mario's world. The sense of scale increases, and the level of complexity attracted both novice and expert players.

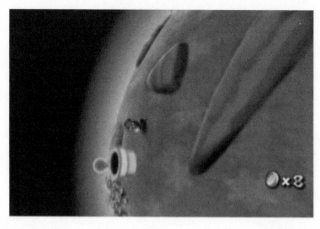

Figure 4.3 Screenshot of *Super Mario Galaxy*.

Super Mario Galaxy continues on this trajectory, increasing a sense of spatial scale again (see Figure 4.3). This new format offers players a sense of worlds rather than just landscapes, visually extending the metaphor of "World 1-1" to the gameplay itself.

The two Mario Galaxy games borrow a number of control schemes from *Super Mario 64* in order to traverse this 3D space. The challenge that Miyamoto and his development team faced was how to employ the Wii Remote to provide players with a simplified control experience for a complex world. The elegance of these Mario titles was the ways in which the use of the Wii Remote and Nunchuk closely mirrored previous Nintendo controllers with minor exceptions (see Figure 4.4).

With the Nunchuk, players are able to move the analog stick and control Mario's directions. The Z button controls Mario's abilities to crouch. Similarly, on the GameCube controller, the player's hand wraps around a short device and uses her left hand to control the analog stick. The primary input button for jumping is the "A" button on the Wii Remote, and on the GameCube, it's the large green button—the largest and most prominent button on both consoles. Those similarities aside, there are some differences in the control schemes. The first is that players have to shake the Wii Remote to use the spin attack

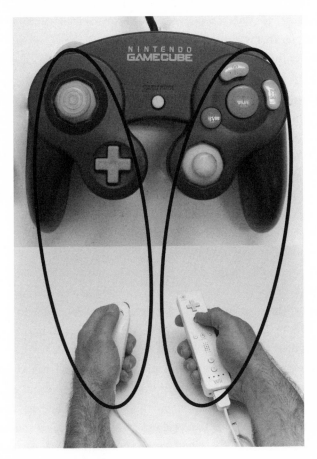

Figure 4.4 Comparing the Nintendo GameCube and Wii Remote controller configurations.

(Photo credit, GameCube controller: Judd Ruggill courtesy of the Learning Games Initiative Research Archive)

(a gameplay mechanism imported from *Super Mario Bros. 3* [1988]). Miyamoto further developed the spin attack in order to increase difficulty and challenge. As Takao Shimizu, one of the producers of the game, explained, "Originally, you were able to spin as much as you wanted. If you kept shaking the Wii Remote, you were able to defeat as many enemies as you liked. But then Miyamoto-san said,

'Let's change it so once you spin, you won't be able to spin again for a little while. That way, you'll learn to time shaking the Wii Remote, and while you can't spin, you'll have to deal with enemy attacks. It would be a lot more fun,' and it became the way it is today" ("A Mario Even Beginners Can Play" n.d.). The second is the use of the star pointer, a small icon that appears on the screen when the Wii Remote is pointed at the screen and allows players to pick up star bits, attach onto pull stars to move through the galaxy, and guide giant bubbles that Mario and Luigi can travel in.

The Super Mario games garnered positive review after positive review; Metacritic gives both 1 and 2 a 97/100. While some reviews have taken the games to task for poor visuals (Reisinger 2007) or being just another Mario game (Welsh 2014), the fact is that Miyamoto has always explained that he doesn't care about the visuals, or about the franchise, or about the story; he cares about gameplay and he puts his creative focus onto innovating gameplay. Thus, Super Mario Galaxy games are iterations on what we know about the Mario universe, and the new twist put into the scheme is the novel use of gravity that affects Mario when he is running and jumping on these small, round worlds. This was not a new idea born from this project. As Iwata explains during one of his Iwata Asks interviews, Miyamoto had been arguing for a gameplay mechanic that explores extreme physics on spheres for some time: "Incidentally, I had heard about the spherical platforms from Miyamoto-san more than five years ago, though at the time, I didn't quite understand why having spherical platforms would be so ground-breaking. However, as Mario Galaxy began to take shape, I finally started to understand" ("How Super Mario Was Born" n.d.).

It is difficult to pinpoint influence in the game industry. Yes, the game is highly rated and continues to be celebrated in games journalism and among developers, but the timing of this game coincided with the rise of the casual game on smart phones and tablets. It may be that the physics manipulation introduced in *Super Mario Galaxy* went on to inspire such games as *Angry Birds Space* (Rovio 2012) or *Cyto* (Room 8, 2014), or it could just be an inspirational family game that people can point to for world building, puzzles, and the feel of the game, for as Melissinos and O'Rourke (2013) write, "*Super Mario Galaxy 2* has no overarching message; rather, it pulls from the heart of the inner child and allows the player to be free to explore fantastical worlds, to delight in discovery, and quite simply, to feel happy while visiting Mario's world" (190).With the bright colors, the stylized creatures and landscapes, and even the cute utterances that Mario exclaims as he moves about the world, *Super Mario Galaxy* continues to evoke childhood, with its playgrounds and challenges. Miyamoto continues to make this landscape available to players both young and old.

While Mario continues its theme in returning to childhood, the Zelda franchise took a different turn. As discussed in Chapter 2, Miyamoto was inspired by his own childhood experiences of exploration. Yet Zelda has always appealed to fans differently from Mario's playgrounds, giving people access to a darker world of dungeons, dangers, and spatial puzzles. Miyamoto started as director, but he turned that position over to Eiji Aonuma and took the role of producer during development. Originally, *Twilight Princess* was intended for the GameCube, but Miyamoto saw an opportunity to use the Wii controllers for aiming and sword fighting. The challenge that faced Miyamoto and Aonuma was that North American audiences, in particular, thought that *The Legend of Zelda: The Wind Waker* (Nintendo 2002) was too childlike because of its cartoonish characters.

The Wind Waker used cell-shading technologies, which made the characters feel more like a cartoon (see Figure 4.5). The response to this in Japan was generally more positive because Japan is a country that consumes manga and anime at all ages. Thus, having a game that borrows from the aesthetics of anime is actually a well-documented practice (deWinter 2009). This is similar to US game developers drawing from television and movies to make aesthetic choices in games, such as using replicating visual motifs from *Saving Private Ryan* (Spielberg 1998) and *Band of Brothers* (Robinson 2001) in such games as *Call of Duty* (Infinity Ward 2003). However, the US

Figure 4.5 Screenshot of *The Wind Waker*, showing the cell-shaded aesthetic.

market's response was less favorable to this choice of a cartoon-like aesthetic. During a Virgin Megastore Roundtable interview, Miyamoto responded to a question regarding whether the cartoonish visual representation in *Wind Waker* would miss its mark in a market that demands realism, explaining: "We have a very popular cartoon movie maker in Japan who is appealing to adults and children alike, and many fans of these animated movies are parents. I don't believe making use of the cartoon style of graphics in *Wind Waker* is any kind of handicap." He reiterated in the same interview that the more difficult challenge is coming up with unique ideas for gameplay ("Virgin Megastore" 2003).

While Miyamoto's point about gameplay is correct, he often undervalues the importance of the visual interface, and we can easily see that here. *Wind Waker* suffered from lackluster sales in the United States (2.6 million units according to VGChartz 2014). Thus, when Nintendo decided to use the Wind Waker engine to make the next Zelda game (originally *Wind Waker 2*), Aonuma went to Miyamoto and asked to do a darker game, one that was more realistic. Miyamoto was dubious; after all, emphasis on the visual over gameplay is almost anathema for him. Yet he collaborated with Aonuma. In recounting an early event during his GDC 2007 presentation, Aonuma explained,

"I was so focused on changing the look of the game as being the solution we were looking for without coming up with a breakthrough game idea, and he advised me that 'If you really want to make a realistic Zelda, you should start by doing what you couldn't in *the Ocarina of Time*. Make it so that Link can attack enemies while riding on his horse using the Wind Waker engine, and make your decision based on how that feels'" (qtd in Kaluszka 2007). From this moment on, Miyamoto would send feedback to the team regarding what it was like to play the game and asking for adjustments.

Throughout the design process of *Twilight Princess*, Miyamoto would often send the team emails that Aya Kyogoku, one of the scenario writers for the game, would call "sob-story emails," or emails in which Miyamoto would tell the team what he tried to do and how the outcome of his efforts were not rewarding enough and thus made him sad ("The Indefinable Essence of Zelda" n.d.). Not only would Miyamoto provide scenario feedback in this way, but he would also provide functional feedback based on his experiences playing the game. For example, he told the team that watching the wolf, Link's form in the Twilight realm, was boring from the back. The team then put a character on the back of the wolf, and while not originally planned, this character became Midna, an essential part of the game ("Ideas Born Out of Functionality" n.d.; see Figure 4.6).

Commenting on this piece of history, Iwata added this observation concerning Miyamoto's approach to game design:

The really interesting thing about what you've just told us is that Miyamoto-san was "speaking from a functional point of view." It wasn't that he wanted a character riding the wolf for narrative reasons. Rather, the reason was to do with its function in the game, as "viewing an animal directly from behind all the time is boring." It's really interesting to hear that the idea of having someone riding the wolf was because of this. I really feel that this is the thinking of someone who worked in industrial design. Sidetracking just a little, when Miyamoto-san got Mario to ride Yoshi in Super Mario World, the thinking behind that idea was "functional." What I mean is that the SNES was a console

Figure 4.6 Screenshot of Midna freeing wolf Link in *Twilight Princess*.

which didn't allow a lot of sprites (the technical mechanism that allows graphics to be displayed on the screen) to be lined up on-screen at the same time. To explain why Yoshi ended up looking like a dinosaur, it's because that shape allows you to limit the number of sprites lined up on screen when Mario and Yoshi are overlapping. ("Ideas Born Out of Functionality")

Iwata sees direct connections between Miyamoto's industrial design training and his video game design aesthetics. His decision to add a character riding the wolf had no original purpose in the game's narrative. Rather, the lack of a character diminished gameplay and a sense of immersion: Miyamoto knows the danger of boredom, and addresses this with puzzles, challenges, and, apparently, interesting things to look at.

In addition to the gameplay and aesthetic choices, Miyamoto saw the potential of Zelda games to fully utilize the Wii Remote. Like the Super Mario Galaxy games, *Twilight Princess* uses both the Wii Remote and the Nunchuk to control Link in a 3D environment. Beyond navigation, these controllers allow the player to simulate swinging a sword by swinging the Wii Remote and to fire arrows and grappling hooks by pointing and firing the Wii Remote. Again, the idea was to marry the player's body and actions to the characters' bodies and actions, and Sinfield's "Living the Hy Life" (2007) provides photographic evidence for the ways that Nintendo envisioned players to use the controllers for the game. For example, in a short segment on the Archery Challenge, a young woman is holding the Wii Remote close to her ear and the Nunchuk component far forward, simulating the stance of drawing a bow (49). For the most part, this worked; when the player swings the sword, Link swings a sword. However, there is little finesse in *Twilight Princess*. Indeed, it wasn't until *The Legend of Zelda: Skyward Sword* that designers were able to add accuracy to Wii Remote swinging in the Zelda games. In other words, it matters how the player swings the sword and how good the aim is in order to hit the enemy during a fight scene.

Twilight Princess launched to much fanfare, and Aonuma's decision to go with a more adult visual theme seemed to be the right call. Steven Grimm's *Nintendo Power* launch article "Link in a New Light: The Zelda Series Goes Where No Link Has Dared: Older, Darker and Much Hairier" celebrates the photorealism and more mature storyline. So while Miyamoto missed the mark on the importance of visuals in the evolving game market, his attention to details through the *Twilight Princess* development process ensured that the team continued to treat the game as a whole rather than component parts. Also, as Aonuma recounted during an Iwata Asks interview that reads like a game postmortem, Miyamoto critiqued parts of the game, reminding Aonuma that they were creating something for people's entertainment ("Focusing on the Player's Perspective" n.d.). Aonuma admitted that this critique made sense and helped to define scope as well as design decisions.

Ultimately, what Miyamoto added to the design of the game, in addition to the player's perspective, was an almost Shakespearian sense of game creation. According to Miyamoto, "it's like setting the scene for a play rather than recreating the world as it is. If you don't tell people they should be making a stage, they go ahead and try to make an entire world" ("A First-rate Link, Even by Nintendo Standards" n.d.). Even in these late games, we see Miyamoto's sense of world building for immersion and transportation. Games don't need realism *per se*;

they need stage setting so that we can be transported by the medium with which we engage. Such an approach has aesthetic consequences in game design, but it also makes good economic sense. As the cost of developing games rises in both price and time, such approaches allow designers to develop key moments in a game more deeply than others while still maintaining player engagement. This stage setting can be seen in *Wii Sports*, a simple game, and it can be seen in *Twilight Princess*, a complex narrative-based game.

Playing as Mii in *Wii Sports* and *Wii Play*

The Wii was released in North America for the 2006 Christmas season, and packaged with the console was *Wii Sports*, a collection of tennis, baseball, bowling, golf, and boxing games. Each of these games would have been a game on its own, but Miyamoto saw potential in these games as a set: together, they would convince families to play Wii every day with a sport for each member of the household ("A Truly Ground-breaking Collection of Games" n.d.). The challenge that Miyamoto and Nintendo designers faced with *Wii Sports* was showcasing the new hardware technology and offering a diverse group of players a game experience that would entertain them and bring them back for more. In the end, *Wii Sports* highlighted not only the hardware technologies, but also the Mii avatars.

Mii avatars are abstracted customizable avatars that can be imported into games as the player character or even just a face in the crowd (see Figure 4.7). The idea of customizable avatars is not new with the Nintendo Wii; people have been customizing avatars in games such as *World Golf Tour* (Nelson and Cheng 2008) and *World of Warcraft* (Blizzard 2004). Nintendo, too, conceived of customizing avatars as early as *Mario Artist: Talent Studio* (2000); the idea was that people could paint a face onto a character. Miyamoto did not give up this idea—it lies at the heart of player-character connection that he always

Figure 4.7 Screenshot of Mii avatars.

strives for. The challenge with the Mii was providing players with customizable options but keeping it simple enough so that the avatars did not unnecessarily tax the system. To this end, Miyamoto drew inspiration from Japanese Kokeshi dolls, simple wooden dolls with limited features (see Figure 4.8). Kokeshi representation, according to Jones and Thiruvathukal, "economize on representation in order to concentrate on other features (such as simulated motions)" (15). In opting for abstract representation, Miyamoto tapped into the potential of abstract images to increase a sense of social connection.

While there are debates about the uncanny valley—a theory that suggests that when representation is too close to the real thing, a feeling of alienness grips the audience, turning them away from the object (normally a humanoid object)—the fact is that extreme realism can create in the player a feeling of distance. Players or audiences might feel that the hair doesn't move correctly or that the skin is strange or that the eyes are just not quite right. Abstract images, on the contrary, are not subject to this type of scrutiny. Further, abstract images enable exaggerated actions and emotions, which make it easier for audience

Figure 4.8 Kokeshi dolls: the inspiration for the Mii avatars.
(Image from Wikimedia Commons: http://commons.wikimedia.org/wiki/File:National_Museum_of_Ethnology,_Osaka_-_Kokeshi_dolls_(Zaôtakayu_type).jpg)

members to read and connect to (deWinter 2009). These avatars matter for connection. As Silverman et al. (2003) argue, on-screen avatars allow fictional characters to stand in for viewers, causing them to slowly accept the avatar as a representation of themselves. Thus, players *become* their avatars rather than simply identifying with them, enabling greater transportation. Miis become a personal representation when playing sports or music, kart-driving, or just hanging out.

And finally, by deemphasizing the visual realism, Miyamoto was able to focus on presenting characters for which the core defining feature was realistic action: the core gameplay experience. For example, when discussing making the *Baseball* game in *Wii Sports* during his 2007 GDC talk, Miyamoto explained that he has always wanted to make a baseball game. He loves baseball. So if there was ever a game that he wanted to be realistic, this was it. Yet President Iwata placed budget and time limitations on him, which Miyamoto interpreted as a call for him to "use his head a little more to problem solve" ("A Creative Vision"). Miyamoto then discussed his prioritization approach: He wanted to give the player a simulated and fun experience pitching and hitting in the game, so the development focus switched to this. The Miis, then, offered an elegant stand-in for the players on the field, and their simplicity did not detract from the pitching and hitting. As Yamashita observed, "The kokeshi might be simple, but your mind helps make it more real. In Wii Sports Baseball, even though the arms and legs aren't shown when the fielders move, it feels realistic when you see them in motion" ("Did Anyone Say It Should Look Realistic?" n.d.). Arguably, the simplicity of the Miis added to the core gameplay experience, which added to the realism, but a realism based in action not in visuals.

Wii Sports as a whole has been a tremendous success for Nintendo and Miyamoto. Early on in the development process, Miyamoto wanted to create a game that would bring players to the Wii console every day, making the Wii the central portal of interaction in everyone's living rooms. The challenge that he faced was how to compel people to log in every day, and for this, he saw the potential of *Wii Sports* and *Wii Play*. Katsuya Eguchi, the producer of *Wii Sports*, explained that Miyamoto guided *Wii Sports* early in the project to achieve this goal. In an Iwata Asks interview, Eguchi discussed the ways in which Miyamoto employed a "health pack" to this end:

> He was trying to push the idea of Wii as a tool at the heart of the living room, connecting families, so that idea was clearly written down. . . . He wrote everything we needed to do on that paper. He roughly divided all of the trial software we had into categories for sports games or games for all the family. Those family-oriented games went on to be included in Wii Play. He also wrote that we should sell those games bundled with the Wii Remote, as well as explaining the way that the calendar on the Message Board would work in conjunction with these games. This was a function aimed at getting people to switch their Wii on every day. When people play Wii Sports or Wii Play, their results are automatically posted on the calendar in the Message Board. Miyamoto-san had broadly outlined functions like this in the plan he wrote down. That single sheet of paper turned out to be the actual starting line for the development of Wii Sports. ("A Truly Ground-Breaking Collection of Games")

Sports seem to be particularly well suited to this type of extrinsic competitive motivation, yet Miyamoto also appears to be drawing from his arcade history to drive competition. By this, I mean that the arcades of the early 1980s offered the leaderboard, that place where people put their three initials to display proudly next to their score. In arcade culture, some players would defend their position, playing until their score topped the leaderboards once again. Automatically posting results to the message board acts in a similar way, creating an electronic record of success broadly defined—success in scores, times played, dedication, accountability, and so forth while also enhancing community. This function will provide the underpinning of *Wii Fit* the following year.

In terms of gameplay, *Wii Sports'* reliance on swinging movements complements the Wii Remote. Sinfield's 2006 review of the Wii and launch games starts with this endorsement: "Nintendo's next console gives you a direct connection to the game, opening the way for interaction at a new level. It looks great. It plays great. And, yeah, it's a whole lot of fun" (33). In this review, Sinfield discusses the fact that the actions mimic the real world, but the Wii presents heightened reality rather than true-to-life actions. For Wii Sports, the controller allows the player to feel the games: "The Baseball exercise mimics the real-life activity of swinging a bat and hitting the ball a country mile. The Golf demo, similarly, has the remote subbing as a golf club. A big swing executes a drive onto the fairway. A short, elbows-outstretched body swaying swing pushes the ball across the green" (36). Miyamoto wanted to design a game that did not just rely on brute strength but rather required players to develop sport styles. Thus, the speed at which the player moves the Wii Remote affects what happens in the game. Not only does this offer the player a better-simulated experience, but this also offers the player with a greater challenge, but a challenge that is low stakes.

These low-stakes challenges are precisely what make *Wii Sports* a good family and party game. Further, this, according to Juul, is precisely what makes the game "a relaxed social game." Juul goes on to write, "popular social games like *Parcheesi* or *Monopoly* generally have large amounts of chance and moderate amounts of depth, making sure the same player does not win every time" (59). In choosing to compare *Wii Sports* to such family board games, Juul is supporting a stance often taken by Miyamoto: Video games should be things that the whole family plays ("Interview: Games Radar" 2002). The virtual environment, as well, gives a sense of communal play. As Jones and Thiruvathukal note, "Even the NPC Miis that cheer in the stands or from the sidelines are meant to be tokens or surrogates for your friends and family or party guests, creating a cartoon version of a social setting within the game space that implies at least the desirability of a corresponding social group in the living room's physical space" (134). This observation turns simulation on its head: *Wii Sports* and *Wii Play* provide communities, which is a type of rhetoric to convince people to have that same community reflected in the home. Should this rhetoric succeed, Miyamoto's vision of communication and interaction with people in and around a video game would be realized. And if it's realized, according to Miyamoto, it's more fun ("Shigeru Miyamoto Roundtable" 2001). Games like this, then, join *Mario Kart* in creating a party atmosphere with the push of a button.

If there is any doubt about whether Miyamoto succeeded in developing a game for the whole family, regardless of age, all one has to do is search YouTube for videos of Wii players, from children to grandmas. What will greet the viewer is video after video of families performing hilarious body movements and whole groups of people smiling. What happens in this situation is unfettered play. As Kasson (1978) noted in his analysis of Coney Island, the body in motion is a spectacle, and the actions of the group are carnivalesque. This is the play spirit in the Huizingan sense where the rules of everyday life, of the civilized, are suspended. As Barbara Ehrenreich (2006) has observed, dancing and ecstatic movement promote communal pleasure and even ecstasy and bliss. Moreover, as Gulick (1911) has rightly pointed out, children in their play and joy have always moved their body and danced in playground games, from London Bridge to

All Around the Mulberry Bush, which contributes to their sense of community and happiness. In searching for gameplay that adds to people's happiness, Miyamoto tapped into the play spirit, marrying the body, the family, the community, and the game into an experience by which people have fun. *Wii Sports* provided the perfect transition for transferring gaming techniques for other health-related programs. Enter here *Wii Fit*.

Wii Fit: Cornering the market on mothers

Nintendo released *Wii Fit* in 2007, one year after the release of the Wii system. To play *Wii Fit*, people had to purchase a kit with the Wii Balance Board. Slightly larger than a bathroom scale, the Balance Board has two main sensors on the left and right that can accurately weigh people and provide feedback on a person's center of balance via the on-screen interface. In addition, people can use the Wii Remote, which senses speed of actions. Using their Mii avatars, people can play minigames or work with a "personalized trainer" to do yoga, aerobics, strength training, or play balance games. The exercises available offer low- and medium-intensity workouts, but the core gameplay mechanism is posture and balance by learning and adapting one's own center of gravity.

If Nintendo and Miyamoto wanted a game that would attract mothers and wives, demographics that Miyamoto often talks about, then *Wii Fit* was it. According to VGChartz (2014), *Wii Fit* saw 22.69 million units sold, with 8.92 in North America alone. *Wii Fit* was also ubiquitously available in places where consumers typically don't think of for video game sales. Not only could people buy it on Amazon.com or in Wal-Mart, but the *Wii Fit* could be seen in the aisles of Babies "R" Us as well, obviously targeting a desired female demographic. The timing for the *Wii Fit* couldn't have been better, with North Americans not only talking more openly about health and obesity, but also having an expectation and acceptance for alternative input devices that have low applicability to other games, such as the guitars for *Guitar Hero* (Harmonix 2005). Here was a health game that compelled players to play by giving constant feedback and tracing trends in individuals' performances and bodies. Then, when people were done with it, the board could be slid neatly under a coffee table or entertainment center cabinet.

Like most things that Miyamoto designs, *Wii Fit* saw its start in Miyamoto's daily life. He tells the story of attending to his weight and health after he turned forty, first by taking up swimming and then by measuring and graphing his weight every day with a bathroom scale ("Introduction" n.d.). So when he first started out thinking through the "health pack"—*Wii Fit*'s original title—the only game mechanism was a daily chart of people weighing themselves. Added to this was an ideal situation that played out in Miyamoto's imagination, that families would weigh themselves together in the living room and talk about their weight and health. To this idea Miyamoto added the ability to record what people ate, but these were the only parameters that he provided his staff at the beginning of development ("Like Nothing Anyone's Done Before"). From there, Miyamoto and his team developed the Balance Board with four sensors, and the increase from two to four sensors enabled the team to move from sports movements to balance-based movements that improve people's center of gravity.

Like *Wii Sports*, *Wii Fit* compels people to turn on the Wii daily in order to do something as simple as weighing themselves. In this way, the Wii console again becomes part of the living room's landscape, central to daily life. However, Miyamoto and his team realized that the challenge lay in getting people to switch from their bathroom scales to the Wii for this part of their daily ritual. If people had to turn on the Wii, find the disk, and insert it, and go through a start-up process, they may be dissuaded from using the Wii in the daily manner that it was intended. To that end, Miyamoto and his team decided quite early that *Wii Fit* would have a dedicated channel so that all people had to do was turn on the Wii and use the network to access their data ("The Importance of Being Aware of One's Body" n.d.). As such, people would be more likely to use *Wii Fit* every day and track the changes in their body. Ultimately, this is the design goal that Miyamoto had. It wasn't to make people more fit; it was to make them more aware of their body, talking with others about their health and well-being ("The Importance of Being Aware of One's Body" n.d.).

While Miyamoto's earlier designs influenced the entertainment gaming industry, this is a game that greatly influences the trajectory of serious games, gamification, and specifically, games for health. The underlying ideology here is that bodies are rational systems and people can be trained through the rewards structure of games to manage those systems. Interestingly, the impact of *Wii Fit* can be seen more clearly in health-related industries over game design industries. While it is true that *Wii Fit* is part of a trajectory of exergames, it is difficult to see the impact of Miyamoto's design choices in the types of games that he included. Rather, *Wii Fit* helped to ensure greater market penetration for the Wii System; people who may not have bought a game system or were ambivalent about which system to buy may have bought the Wii because they wanted the *Wii Fit*, and enough online community evidence in the forms of blogs and forums supports this supposition. Yet further evidence of the *Wii Fit* opening up market niches can be seen in health studies and the health industry. Studies abound that examine *Wii Fit*'s use for children's physical activity (Baranowski et al. 2012; Vernadakis et al. 2012), the physical well-being of adults and families (Owens et al. 2011; Nitz et al. 2010), and its usefulness in helping the sick or the elderly improve balance and health (Padala et al. 2012; Plow and Finlawson 2011). Consistent throughout these studies is a technological approach to exercise. Only briefly touched on in most of these articles, however, is the psychological motivation for exercise and well-being, and this is what Miyamoto brought to exergames as a game designer: thirty years of game design that offers players an experience that they will find fun and rewarding.

Conclusion

The Wii console saw a spotlight shine on Nintendo in a way that hadn't happened since the 1980s, and in that spotlight, Miyamoto's designs were all the more highlighted. It would be a misnomer to label Miyamoto's games and Wii games in general as part of the casual game movement. Yes, there are plenty of examples of casual games, such as *Wii Sports* and some of the minigames on *Wii Fit*; however, *Wii Fit*, I would argue, is not a casual game in its entirety. *Wii Fit* takes long-term investment, logging in every day in order to see trends in health. Further, these trends ideally will make people adapt the habits of their life, and those habitual changes will be rewarded via the *Wii Fit* interface. *Super Mario Galaxy*, too, is both a casual game and a game that requires skill and training. Ultimately, *Super Mario Galaxy* evokes childhood to compel players to explore and play around, delighted at everything that they see. And then all a person needs to look to is the Wii Zelda games to understand that the Wii is not only a casual platform. The complexity and maturity of these two Zelda games is still celebrated.

What the Wii games make clear yet again is Miyamoto's dedication as a businessman who works in both hardware and software development. He helped to design the Wii and controller scheme. He then designed games that highlighted the capabilities of the Wii, modeling for other developers what could be done. Furthermore, he expanded his markets by creating social games that attracted families and social groups. The Wii platform and the games that he created for it are another instantiation of his early design philosophies: games are for fun, community, and communication; hardware creates a direct connection between the player and the actions on the screen; Nintendo is a business for entertainment and profit.

5

In His Own Words: Transcript of Miyamoto's 1999 Game Developer Conference Keynote

In 1999, Shigeru Miyamoto was invited to give the keynote speech at the US Game Developer's Conference at the Civic Auditorium in San Jose California. This particular keynote address speaks to many of the themes included in this book. Thus, while some of the examples seem dated (this is the Nintendo 64 era), I have chosen this keynote because Miyamoto speaks about both hardware and game design. He especially emphasizes the challenges of designing gameplay and his particular focus on what he calls "user reactions"—Miyamoto is dedicated to giving players a fun and immersive experience, and this talk speaks to some of the strategies that he employs. Here in one speech, we can see evidence of a game designer speaking of his vision and philosophy and how these affect his approaches to designing systems of experiences.

Good Evening! Thank you very much for your warm welcome. I am very happy to be here.

The video game industry has been through many crises, yet, has continued on as a strong and growing business. Thanks to that, I am still making games, and I get to speak to you about them today. I owe a lot to a number of people who have been involved in this business—and also to the newcomers in this industry who have grown up playing Nintendo games and continue to purchase them today.

Making use of this opportunity, I'd like to speak about my own experiences for the past twenty years. If what I tell you today can help games to consistently be fun to play, it would make me happy. In fact, I like making games so much that I would do it for free, but don't tell

Mr Yamauchi that! And now, I hope you will do me a big favor and allow me to speak in Japanese. My friend, Bill Trinen, will translate for me. There are three main topics I'd like to speak about today:

Looking back at the history of game designing. And what I think game designing should be. Ideas behind the creation of *Zelda 64*. My policy toward future creations.
(Japanese translation begins at this point):

Until the time of *Donkey Kong*, which was the first game I directed, programming and hardware engineers were responsible for game design. Those were the days when these engineers were even composing the music and drawing the pictures themselves (resulting in rather primitive, now classic, games). When I, as a graphic designer, first became involved in game design, I used to boast to myself that I was one of the five best game designers in the world, since there were few designers with artistic experience in game design back then.

Donkey Kong and other games gave birth to a new trend in which video games had an accompanying story for the first time, and the work of game designers came to include drawing the pictures and writing the story. This trend continued for approximately ten years, during which time many designers joined the industry, and professional music composers also began to take a role in game design.

Then, due particularly to the success of *Dragon Warrior* and *The Legend of Zelda* in Japan, there emerged a new trend in which scenario writers took leading roles in game design. At this time I was inundated by many designers-to-be hoping to get their scenarios turned into games, and we also saw popular scenario writers teaming up with music composers in the hopes of churning out a game for the sake of business.

And in recent years, as I predicted, advancements in technology have once again brought programmers and engineers to the forefront of game design, and we are now in an age in which we cannot accomplish anything new without these individuals.

Let us look back once again. In the days since I have joined the industry, we have also seen a qualitative change in the nature of game play. Early on, the objective of arcade style games was to see how many quarters we could get users to drop into the machines. It was with this goal in mind that we created the *Donkey Kong* series, but at the same time we encountered problems with new types of games that contradicted this model. One example is baseball, in which you must play nine innings to complete a game, but at a quarter an inning one game is too expensive, while from the point of view of the arcade operator, players could get more play time for a 25 cent inning of baseball than they could on other games. Another example is our *Mario Brothers*, in which the players' objective was to defeat their opponent, but the better they got at the game, the shorter their play time lasted. Players had a hard time accepting these types of game concepts.

It was at this time that I became involved in the development of the Nintendo Entertainment System, which offered us an environment outside of the arcade for which we could create games. We put higher priority on developing two hand-held controllers rather than a single, ultrafunctional controller to open the door to games like baseball and *Mario Bros*. With the NES, the business of selling game play time transformed completely and evolved into the business of simply selling game play.

Throughout these changes I have maintained the same style of game design. Although I am not an engineer, I have always included in my designs consideration for the technology that will make those designs a reality. People have paid me a lot of lip service, calling me a genius story teller or a talented animator, and have gone so far as to suggest that I try my hand at movies, since my style of game design is, in their words, quite similar to making movies. But I feel that I am not a movie maker, but rather that my strength lies in my pioneering spirit to make use of technology to create the best, interactive commodities possible and use that interactivity to give users a game they can enjoy and play comfortably.

I feel that I have been very lucky to be a game designer since the dawn of the industry. I am not an engineer, but I have had the opportunities to learn the principles of game from scratch, over a long period of time. And because I am so pioneering and trying to keep at the forefront, I have grown accustomed to first creating the very tools necessary for game creation. I have seen both the evolution of hardware and the advent of hit software titles, but I have seen that not all the ideas for new hardware development come from engineers and hardware professionals. And I have seen more than a few examples in which the idea for a hit title has popped out of a simple conversation with an ordinary person.

Recently, I have encountered many instances in which we hit a brick wall in game development and never quite make it to completion. I believe many of you have at one time or another found yourself in the same boat, and may have even had no choice but to release a game to market in an incomplete or unsatisfactory condition, much to your own mortification.

I am sure that each case has its own unique cause, but I know that when (Nintendo's) game designers and producers make their plans without a sufficient grasp of the technology and engineering necessary to make their game, they will often fail. Also, we may be frustrated to find that a game we are developing never really becomes fun to play no matter how hard we try to improve it. Recently, when new technology and exquisite graphics are regarded as the core of a game's element of fun, it becomes difficult to evaluate a game before launch, because those fun aspects of it can only be judged after everything is in order and the game is nearly complete. So the answer to the question of how many more months of tinkering will produce a truly enjoyable game depends upon a variety of newly emerging technologies. Until the technology is complete, game designers are unable to evaluate how enjoyable the game will be, and because that level of enjoyment is dependent upon the level of completion of that technology, there is no guarantee that the final game will be enjoyable at all.

In my understanding, game designers are solely to blame in these situations. But, on the other hand, since there is no concrete definition of what a game designer's work entails, I cannot say that it really is the fault of the designers. As I mentioned earlier, in the history of game development, there was a time when designers were engineers who were less capable of composing sound and creating exquisite graphics. Then we had designers who were painters, but could not understand the technology behind the games. They didn't know what they could and could not do. How were they to express their ideas so that they could be understood by programmers and realized by the CPU? Later, scenario writers took the lead, but they, too, had a low level of understanding of the technology.

Fortunately, because I have been a part of the industry since its dawning, I have at last come to the conclusion that the role of a game designer is to design a complete game system by first comprehending the technologies that will enable and realize that system.

I believe that design itself is one of the jobs of a game designer. How will the ideas I have in my mind be reproduced by the computer? How can the power of the CPU be best allotted in order to convey those ideas to the user? Will the players always be able to find fun and enjoyment from this game? How can I bring my own constructions and expression of ideas together with the technology that creates that new level of enjoyment within the hardware and budget limitations placed upon me? This is what I mean by design.

I consider games to be entertainment commodities and therefore place great importance on user reaction. I realize that I am one of those users to be monitored when I play a new game for the first time. It is important to design the whole game creation process so that users' needs will be reflected effectively and quickly at the time of completion, and this is why game directors must be deeply involved in the design process.

Accordingly, in our company, all designers must go through technical training. Graphic designers make games by comprehending the ROM and RAM memory maps. Which specialists are taking the lead in design depends on the current trends, but this technical training is a basic requisite for continued success in game design.

Let me offer you some examples. Suppose a director presented the following game specification for an action game. "The enemy shall randomly search and react to the character." To randomly search may sound like an appropriate specification, but a programmer cannot program this as it is, and in the latter stages of development, the director won't know what to begin with when trying to bring the game close to its original concept. But what if the specification presented was "The enemy shall change course based on character movement once every 30 game frames, and one in three times it will randomly select to progress in"? This should be more easily programmed than the previous example; we will know where to begin modifying, if necessary.

In a best case scenario, you may be teamed up with talented programmers, and the programmers may be able to make the game on their own and have it turn out to be quite enjoyable. In such cases, I may no longer be necessary, and programmers can make the whole game on their own. Honestly, I have been very fortunate in that I always seem to be joined by a group of excellent programmers.

The next necessary element of design is skillful management of the memory map and accurate estimation of the processing speed. When we make games for consumer game consoles, it is important to take into account the limited ability, processing speed, and transfer rate of the console. For users and company management who do not have a technical grounding, it is taken for granted that the virtual world exists in the game. This is a matter of course. If we see a man running and there is a hill in front of him, naturally, he will run up the hill. If a car is bearing down on him, we can guess that it will hit him. We assume that the car's wheels will turn when the car is moving and stop turning when the car stops. For the users and management, these are the laws of nature, but they don't realize that we are the ones who have created this virtual world. When problems arise in the end, they ask "Can't you do this? Does the processing speed have to be so slow? Why do I have to wait so long at this point?" But at that stage of development, such areas cannot be fixed. When we were making games for the NES, sounds in the game consumed CPU power, so in early development we would include dummy sounds so that we could estimate the processing speed of the final product. There were days when we were playing Super

Mario Bros. to the music of Excite Bike, and Mario's jump didn't have its characteristic "boing," but rather the rev of a motorbike. This kind of consideration is necessary for taking the interface into account and in order for us to focus our attention on the areas of the game that we have placed our creative priorities on.

Also, in many cases, we miscalculate the time necessary to prepare parts of the game that are often taken for granted. The less experience a designer has, the easier it is to make this mistake. But the amount of programs and sequences which are unique to any given game are actually quite limited, and represent less than a third of the total. Taking the example of an RPG, there are countless features that are taken for granted, such as the title and name registration screens, the dialogue system, item select windows, and so on. I call these parts "labor," and I am always trying to design games which feature as few of these parts as possible. Unfortunately, many game blueprints contain a number of these elements, and it is often work on these "labor" elements exceeding our time estimations that lead to the troubles of games not reaching completion.

With this in mind, we can reduce this labor by creating an entirely new genre of games that no one has ever thought of before, right?

Though I have talked mostly about the technical aspects of game design, I would now like to talk about something on the opposite end of the spectrum. We must not forget the importance of human ingenuity and creativity in game design. Naturally, it is new and unique expression of ideas that gives birth to new games. Recently, I am very sorry to see that the uniqueness of many titles has been dependent upon new technology and specialty development tools, while the personalities of the creators have been diluted. For me, game creation is like expression through music. When I am working as a director on a game, while I always try to hit upon new plots, I place great importance on the tempo of the game and the sound effects. I feel that those directors who have been able to incorporate rhythm and emotional stimuli in their games have been successful. When I am holding the controller and setting the tempo, I feel that my own personal game is in the midst of creation. I have never created a game that has been of a level that I could be satisfied with. Understanding the technologies is the requisite if we want to fully realize our expression. Game designers are apt to boast of the technical aspects of their games, and I, too, have fallen into this trap. Speaking of my own case, I tend to highlight new technologies when I am less confident about the new ideas I am putting forward in the game, and later, I always regret doing this. It is important for us to remember that technology can inspire new ideas and help us realize those ideas, but it should do so from the background.

Next, I'd like to discuss a game that I recently worked on, which you may or may not have heard of.

We started with about four or five different teams, each working on basic experiments related to game design.

1. Scenario and Planning—both very necessary. The team discussed the position of this title in the whole series and included myself and several dedicated script writers.
2. Link's action and 3D improvements of items found previously in the series: This team included myself; Mr Yoshiaki Koizumi, who has worked on player characters since the days of Mario; and the head programmer. Mr Koizumi is here in the audience this evening. Where are you? If you happen to see him at the conference, say hello. He may share some useful information with you.
3. A variety of camera experiments were conducted by the same team that handled Link's action plus several designers and programmers. We worked on incorporating new methods, such as background virtual boxes which we did not use in Mario, as well as fixed camera modes like we used in the castle.
4. Another team worked on bringing the items that Link touches and uses that lay at the basis of the game, into the 3D world.
5. Motion-capture production and tests for the creation of the converter used in the Zelda's animation, which was done by an entirely different team.

We also formed new teams according to our needs. There was the Sound team: Ocarina play and 3D sound, special effects. The flow of time in the background and background culling appropriate for Zelda. What was unique here was not just what was visible in the background, but progressing with design and integration of terrain-specific sound and movement, camera moves, and enemy data and tools effective for manipulating this data.

We designed the entire game by organizing these small teams and conducting tests to confirm memory size and processing speed. Let us recall Hyrule Field in *The Legend of Zelda*. The characters that appear in the field all share RAM. So, following the scenario, we have the great bird, Gebola, and the Skeleton enemies, and then once the bird has left the field, the Marathon Man appears. When Link rides the horse as an adult, the only enemy to appear is the ghost. So the scenario is written to match these types of design specifications.

I would like to add that depending on the type of game we may start development with just the character's movement, and of course not all experiments will be adopted in the final game.

These are the technical aspects of Zelda's development. Let me now talk about the concepts behind the game. Through our experience of making this interactive media called video games, we have uncovered a number of methods to stimulate a player's emotion. One way is through the use of cinematic sequences. As you know, seeing with one's own eye can give a more pronounced effect than a player's imagination. With that, let's take a look at some of Zelda's cinema scenes.

We have seen several examples of these cinema scenes, but we positioned these sequences as only one part of development. In Zelda, there are over 1 hour and 30 minutes of cinema scenes. But the staff involved in creating these scenes was only three individuals for most of the development process, and in the latter stages, only six or seven. The reason behind using such a simple process, as I am sure you have all experienced in the workshop, is that there is a total limit on team energy. There is a limit to the work a team can do, and there is a limit to my own energy. We opted not to use that limited time and energy on prerendered images for use in cinema scenes, but rather on tests on other interactive elements and polishing up the game to create a product that players can enjoy and play comfortably. Actually, I changed the scenario just a few months before completion, and although the staff was rather unhappy about taking apart something they had already created, we were able to make the fixes in a short amount of time, so that it did not cause any problems time-wise. It is not because the N64 doesn't have access to a CD-Rom that we incorporated real-time movie processing. Quite the contrary, to the greatest extent possible we were able to make use of truly cinematic methods with our camera work without relying on the kind of data typically used to make cinema scenes.

Our president, Mr Yamauchi, says that each product has its own mission. We set interactivity as the mission for our products. And thanks to that, we were able to experience development that no one had experienced before.

I have talked about several different topics this evening, but now I would like to discuss the future of game design.

Shall I begin making *Zelda* for our next generation hardware? At this point, the answer to that question is no. The reason for my saying this is that all of the elements for which Zelda has received so much praise for had already been incorporated into the game more than a year before completion, when I felt the game was not fun to play. I think that a lot of the reasons that Zelda has been so praised are not related to the N64's level of expression, the unique camera systems and auto-jump system, nor the gorgeous cinema scenes and spectacular boss fights. It is true that some other team may realize the level of expression that we achieved with Zelda, but of course it will not be the exact same as Zelda. With improved hardware, I can imagine Zelda having more detailed graphics and a quicker response time, but when it comes to increasing the degree of fun, I cannot be certain of that at this time. This is something that I feel we as designers must reconsider.

Also, I want to constantly make efforts to create new ideas. I want to propose new game ideas without worrying about the headaches of management, such as inflated development costs. Video games have become far more popular than in the past, but I feel that we have just been repeating the same events again and again in this unique market. Even with Zelda I did not feel that sense of freshness that I had with the original *Super Mario Bros.* I want to make efforts to convey the charm of video games to the general public that is currently outside the reach of the industry in which we do business. This is because I really want to feel the unique zest of the entertainment industry, where one simple idea can create an unexpected social phenomenon.

Let's take a look at a game I am working on now called *Talent Maker.*

What you are seeing now is a newly born *Mario Paint*, a new game in which you can create your own characters by utilizing the Game Boy camera, and you can make those characters dance and what have you. The scenes you have seen, including one in the introduction, were made very quickly by my staff using this software. Nintendo will also make efforts to create new types of commodities by combining the Game Boy, the Game Boy Camera, the Rumble Pak, and others with the N64. In Japan, we have already launched the N64 title *Pokémon Stadium*, which makes use of the Game Boy *Pokémon* games, and we are selling *Pikachu Genkidenchu*, an N64 game which employs voice recognition technology. Soon we will introduce a new system, in which the Game Boy can be used as a controller for the N64.

We have expanded this industry and welcomed new users with innovative products that continue to surprise us. At a time when we were all developing *Mario*-style scrolling games, *Tetris* was born thanks to a team that tried to make a new product with Game & Watch style software. When we were stuck on talk of the spectacular 3D graphics of *Mario 64* and racing games, we saw a huge hit in the form of Tamagochi—a tiny keychain boasting pictures made up of no more than ten or twenty dots. At that time, I thought that *Mario 64* had lost to Tamagochi.

I want game designers to be the designers who make technology their tools, and use it to express their own individuality, their own uniqueness, and their own rhythm, as well as the entertainers who make this world a more enjoyable one. It is with this extravagant hope that I wish to end my speech.

My friends, let us design unique, fun software with new appeal. Let us take on new challenges so that the world of gaming is not left behind as a separate, closed off world. And in the process, let's see if we can't make a little money.

6

A Continuing Legacy

Miyamoto's game design career has spanned a number of changes in the industry, from arcades to home and handheld consoles, and also through a number of innovations in hardware and software. What is remarkable about Miyamoto is that his design vision has stayed fairly consistent since his early designs. Over his career, though, Miyamoto has more strongly aligned himself with gameplay and joy as his guiding philosophies and has moved away from his manga and puppet-show narrative beginnings. This shift has allowed him to expand his inspirational source materials from manga and anime to other parts of his life, like gardening and dog ownership. Furthermore, he is able to translate his joy and his observations from these hobbies to create interactive game environments for millions to share. Thus, if the idiom is true—game designers turn experiences into systems— then Miyamoto is an expert game designer, conveying a wide range of experiences into his systems. Then, when people play those games, turning systems back into experiences, we see the fruits of a master at work. Videos of people playing Miyamoto games show delight, happiness, concentration, and that elusive sense of fun. Indeed, during his 2007 GDC talk "A Creative Vision," Miyamoto showed videos of people playing his games, and he explained that the players' delights were his: He succeeded in his goal.

The challenge now while talking about Miyamoto as an influential game designer is that this is typically a retrospective done at the end of a person's career. However, Miyamoto is still designing and producing; his influence can still be strongly felt in Nintendo. And this conclusion becomes even more complicated by the fact that Miyamoto has been called upon to design games in order to save the

Wii U (Crecente 2014; Taylor 2014). The Wii U has had flagging sales since its release at the end of 2012. According to VGChartz, the Wii U has sold only 6.91 million units. Compare this to the sales numbers for Wii consoles (101.05 million units) and DS handheld devices (154.88 million units), and the poor performance of the Wii U is startling in contrast (VGChartz, "Platform Totals" 2014).

Miyamoto and others at Nintendo have been faced with poor-performing consoles in the past. In this instance, however, Miyamoto has been particularly called upon to act as a designer on a number of games, including a new *Star Fox*, and two others tentatively titled *Project Guard* and *Project Giant Robot*. According to Gibson, who live-tweeted a Nintendo shareholder event in Tokyo, "Nintendo's game design guru Shigeru Miyamoto promised that the company is building a 'flagship title' to demonstrate the power of its quality of life platform" (Nutt 2014). This platform adapts much of the success of the DS and its touch screen to the living room console, offering players a multiscreen interface for gameplay in much the same way as the DS. What the Wii U does is allow players to play in the same room while having access to different screens. Thus, in games like *Luigi's Ghost Mansion*, one of the minigames included in *Nintendo Land* (Nintendo 2012), five people can play in one room. Four play as ghost hunters staring at the television screen and holding flashlights to hunt a ghost (they cannot see the ghost without the flashlight shining on the character). The fifth person plays as the ghost, running amok on the Wii U GamePad, invisible to the other players while all players are visible to the ghost player. Subjectively, this is a fun game. Indeed, in her review of *Nintendo Land*, Drake (2012) writes, "The attractions themselves offer ample variety and are ridiculously, unabashedly entertaining. Every play session I've had, no matter the size of the group, always resulted in an eruption of laughter and good times." The problem doesn't seem to be in the quality of these social games, yet Nintendo continues to struggle with the image of the Wii U. Gamers seem to interpret Wii U as a children's only console or a console for only social games. This perception damages Nintendo's standing in the game communities, and both Miyamoto and

President Iwata have worked to bridge the gap between perceptions of core and casual gamers ("Deeper and Wider" n.d.).

The problem with conflating Miyamoto with Nintendo is that when Nintendo struggles, people assume that Miyamoto has lost it. The supposition is that his games and approaches to game design belong to a different era and that he has run his creative course. In his *Eurogamer* article, "Iwata Isn't Nintendo's Problem. It's Miyamoto," Welsh (2014) argues that Nintendo holds tightly to Miyamoto's IPs instead of creating new ones, and that Nintendo needs fresh IPs to stay viable in the contemporary video game market. He writes about Miyamoto, "He's a star that cannot be outshone, and his original creations have become needs to be serviced by those who follow him, rather than inspirations for them to find their own voices." And this is, according to Welsh, what's holding new talent back at Nintendo. Yet Nintendo is in a precarious position as well because they have such a large fan base that they have to serve those people. Fan management has been a successful strategy for Nintendo since its earliest days with dedicated magazines and events. Thus, their resources and Miyamoto's creative influence are demanded in multiple sectors.

In addition to the challenges above, the simple fact is that the video game industry is a volatile industry staffed by relatively young workers. While Nintendo has had long success and stability, the company has also had a number of misses in their developments, such as the Nintendo Power Glove and even, arguably, the GameCube. Yet Nintendo finds ways to define niches in the market and design games for those groups, and Miyamoto's approach to game design successfully compliments these corporate strategies. The other challenge that Miyamoto faces is simply age; in an industry where the average age of workers is between thirty-one and thirty-five (ESA Canada 2013; Kaining 2007), Miyamoto is in his sixties. The video game industry is not like other creative industries where the directors, authors, and artists gain a level of venerability with age. Rather, because the video game industry defines itself as young, the assumption is that only youth talent can tap into the pulse of this popular culture. Yet here again, we see that

Miyamoto brings new perspectives to game design based on his interests and concerns as a more mature person, translating gardening and health management into gameplay and thereby extending his audience beyond this "core" group of gamers.

The above may read as an apology for Miyamoto, a defense of a person who is simultaneously praised for his influence and dismissed because his influence may be waning. What the current debates do not take into account is Miyamoto's projects that reach beyond the traditional gaming industry yet are close to the core mission of Nintendo. For example, in "One day, the Louvre" (n.d.), Iwata talks with Miyamoto about translating another of his hobbies—visiting museums—into an interactive experience. Shortly after the release of the DS, Miyamoto tried to think of ways to use the small handheld device as a guide for events or places, and other companies had the same thought. Nintendo was contracted to make DS-based guides for Ikspiari, a shopping mall inside the Tokyo Disney Resort, and once this project was competed, Nintendo released the *Make It Yourself: Nintendo DS Guide* software (2010) for others to create their own guide programs. Then Miyamoto was called upon to create The Nintendo 3DS Guide: Louvre (Nintendo 2013) for the Louvre museum in France. The software provides audio commentary, maps, the ability to zoom in, and additional contextual information.

The Louvre Guide calls upon Miyamoto's particular skills in creating interactive experiences that are spatially defined. Further, one can only suppose that the user base for the DS program at the Louvre would not be the typical person who went to buy the new Pokémon game (although it can include that person as well). By taking up this project with such a prestigious partner, Miyamoto is once again showing the possibilities of Nintendo hardware for both consumers and other producers. While I do not think that Miyamoto believes that the Louvre guide will significantly expand the Nintendo market, he does see possibilities for using this type of program and even the Louvre guide in art classes for educational purposes ("A Wondrous Experience" n.d.). So while the Wii U games are still much anticipated at the time of writing this book, the fact is that Miyamoto's influence continues to be felt beyond the constraints of the video game industry.

This is not to suggest that Miyamoto does not still exert influence within his own industry. He is consistently included on lists of the most influential game designers in the industry and is often referred to as "the undisputed king" (Darrell 2014). His influence on user interaction and user experience design is being discussed in non-video-gaming magazines (see, for example, "The Legend of Miyamoto: How Nintendo Shaped UX" by Snyder 2012). In 2007, *Time* listed Miyamoto as one of the top 100 people in the world, and Johnathan Wendel, who wrote the honorary article, credits Miyamoto for changing his life and inspiring him to become a professional video gamer. As Whitehead (2012) so succinctly concludes in his tribute of Miyamoto's sixtieth birthday—after equating Miyamoto as a slightly nicer Steve Jobs in the workplace—"The modern video game industry will always owe a great deal to Shigeru Miyamoto, and will do well to heed the philosophies that have made him its foremost figure."

Those philosophies have a lot to do with an understanding of play as a concept that should be safe and enjoyable. The player should not have to work to achieve what the designer wants. The designer should create worlds for the player to enact his or her imagination and provide affordances for multiple types of play. Some of that play will serve the purposes of the game, achieving the goals with high scores. Some of that play will just make everyone in the living room laugh and talk. This is another of Miyamoto's philosophies: play is about community. Play should bring people together, either to coplay or to talk about play experiences. Furthermore, play is inextricably linked to spaces—either spaces in games for exploration or spaces in our daily lives in which our play occurs. As a designer, Miyamoto designs play for spaces, for bodies in those spaces, and for the joy of exploring spaces. And finally, Miyamoto's work suggests that play is innocent, almost childlike. In his early work, he returns to his own childhood for inspiration, and in his later works, he maintains that same joy and carefree movement for the most part. This may allow some to dismiss Miyamoto's work from a growing cannon of serious and mature games. But play as a goal is important; it is seriously important, for as Sutton-Smith reminds us in *The Ambiguity of Play*, the opposite of play is not work, it's depression (1997, 198). It is hard to imagine being depressed when playing a *Mario* game or taking care of your dogs in *Nintendogs*. These are not games that explore darker human emotions.

Much has been written in this book about particular strategies and approaches; however, Miyamoto is at heart a designer of play. Miyamoto creates worlds and populates those worlds with fantastical characters that help to transport the player into a frivolous space. Yet frivolity does not negate seriousness, as Sutton-Smith reminds us. Play is universal in its role in human behavior (Sutton-Smith 1997, 208) and is serious for all groups who play. What Miyamoto gives us is a structure for play via the medium of the video game. In giving us this structure, he shares his own experiences at play while also giving people a shared space, a shared playground, for the formation of play experiences and memories. Important to note is that Miyamoto's design influence extends beyond the game industry; he has spent his career influencing culture writ large. People can go to the symphony and hum along with *Super Mario Bros.*'s theme music; they can go to the movie theaters to watch *The King of Kong* (Gordon 2007) and root for one man's quest to gain the highest score in *Donkey Kong*; they can make post-it note pixel art on the windows of college dormitories, recreating their favorite Nintendo characters. And they can reminisce on the experience of playing these games as children and play these games again and again to recapture some of those initial experiences in an always-accessible playspace.

Gameography

Written with Nicholas DeMarinis

Miyamoto has been in the game industry since the late 1970s in a variety of capacities. For example, before designing *Donkey Kong* (1981), Miyamoto did cabinet design for *Sheriff* (1979), *Space Firebird* (1980), and *Radar Scope* (1980). We do not intend to undervalue this contribution; cabinet design is an important paratext in a game's experience. This gameography, however, only attends to the video games for which Miyamoto influenced game design. Further, one of the challenges of compiling this gameography is the company structure of Nintendo. As Miyamoto has explained, his titles in Nintendo have been *kacho* and *bucho*, or section chief and department chief. People abroad did not understand these titles, so he arbitrarily gave himself other titles, like designer or producer ("Interview: Tokyo University Lecture" 2003). As such, credit in this gameography represents our efforts to translate some of Miyamoto's less-known credits into US-equivalent titles.

A quick comment about this gameography: We have only provided brief descriptions of games in cases where Miyamoto is listed as a designer or a concept creator. We only include basic game information, such as title, platform, and sales figures (when available). Unless otherwise noted, all sales figures provide numbers for units sold and are derived from VGChartz. What becomes obvious when consolidating Miyamoto's contributions in one list is that this is a designer who has touched some of the most recognizable IPs in video game history. Furthermore, almost all of these games have been available on multiple platforms, released constantly through the history of Nintendo. We have chosen to include only initial release information for the purposes of this gameography.

Early Designs

Devil World	NA: 0 JP: 1984 EU: 1987
Platform: Famicom	**Role:** Designer
Sales: N/A	**Franchise:** Early Designs

Most likely inspired by Miyomoto's high regard for *Pac-Man*, *Devil World* is a maze game. Unlike Pac-Man, however, the small green dragon avatar cannot eat the pellets on the screen unless he first picks up a cross. Once the green dragon picks up the cross, he can eat the pellets and breathe fire at the monsters on the screen. Meanwhile, a devil character at the top of the screen is directing his minions, telling them to move the outer walls that frame the accessible parts of the maze. If the green dragon is caught between the frame wall and a maze wall, the character is squished and the player loses a life. Only after collecting four bibles will the player be allowed to progress to the next maze.

Excitebike	NA: 1985 JP: 1984 EU: 1986
Platform: Nintendo Entertainment System	**Role:** Designer
Sales: 4.16M	**Franchise:** Early Designs

Excitebike is a side-scrolling racing game with motocross racing bikes. The player races against other bikes and against a time limit, managing a race course that has a number of jumping ramps. Players must manage the heat of their bikes—if the motor becomes overheated, then the bike stalls for several seconds. In addition to racing, *Excitebike* has a design mode where players can design their own racetracks for play.

Donkey Kong

Donkey Kong	NA: 1981 JP: 1981
Platform: Arcade	**Role:** Designer/Director
Sales: Approximately 60,000 (Kent)	**Franchise:** Donkey Kong

Miyamoto's first game, *Donkey Kong* repurposed *Radar Scope* cabinets and controllers to provide players with a platform game experience. Jumpman must climb a 100-meter tower in 25-meter increments to save Lady from Donkey Kong, a large gorilla who has kidnapped Lady. Miyamoto introduced narrative, contiguous levels, and a jump mechanic in this game. Players can move up the screen using ladders and elevators and must evade falling objects. The game provided Nintendo with a firm foothold into the North American continent. When the game was later adapted to Game & Watch, Miyamoto's mentor Yokoi introduced the D-pad.

Donkey Kong Jr.	NA: 1982 JP: 1982 EU:
Platform: Arcade	**Role:** Designer/Director
Sales: not available	**Franchise:** Donkey Kong

Similar to *Donkey Kong*, *Donkey Kong Jr.* is a four-level platformer in which Junior must save his father Donkey Kong from the cage in which Mario has entrapped him. The player must move up the screen, evading Snapjaws, Nitpickers, and Sparks to collect keys and eventually unlock the cage. Players can climb and slide down vines to travel vertically. This game recycles old Donkey Kong characters and inverts the protagonist and antagonist to make both characters playable and launching two parallel Nintendo franchises.

Donkey Kong 3	NA: 1984 JP: 1984 EU: 1985
Platform: Arcade	**Role:** Director
Sales: not available	**Franchise:** Donkey Kong

This game is almost a classic shooter other than that Stanley, the protagonist of this game, must shoot bug spray to drive Donkey Kong back or to destroy the bugs that are threatening Stanley's flowers. This is a good example of designing a game within the constraints of classic violent games yet redirecting the experience into something that does not feel violent or malicious (as discussed in Chapter 3).

Donkey Kong Country	NA: 1994 JP: 1994 EU: 1994
Platform: Super Nintendo Entertainment System	**Role:** Producer
Sales: 9.30M	**Franchise:** Donkey Kong

Donkey Kong 64	NA: 1999 JP: 1999 EU: 1999
Platform: Nintendo 64	**Role:** Producer
Sales: 5.27M	**Franchise:** Donkey Kong

Donkey Konga	NA: 2004 JP: 2003 EU: 2004
Platform: GameCube	**Role:** Producer/Supervisor
Sales: 1.15M	**Franchise:** Donkey Kong

Donkey Kong Jungle Beat	NA: 2005 JP: 2004 EU: 2005
Platform: GameCube	**Role:** Producer
Sales: 1.34M	**Franchise:** Donkey Kong

Donkey Kong Country Returns	NA: 2010 JP: 2010 EU: 2010
Platform: Wii	**Role:** Supervisor
Sales: 6.19M	**Franchise:** Donkey Kong

Mario

Mario Bros.		NA: 1983 JP: 1983 EU: 1986
Platform: Nintendo Entertainment System/Arcade	**Role:** Designer/Director	
Sales: 2.28M	**Franchise:** Mario	

Mario Bros. is a two-player platform arcade game in which players can play either Mario or his brother Luigi to defeat a constant onslaught of creatures emerging from the sewer systems. Miyamoto imported the jump mechanic for this game and allowed players to fall from great heights without getting hurt. Introduced in this game was the ability to attack foes from beneath by jumping up and hitting the underside of a level and then pushing those characters. (Players cannot yet jump on enemies to kill them unless those enemies are already turned over.)

Super Mario Bros.		NA: 1985 JP: 1985 EU: 1987
Platform: Nintendo Entertainment System	**Role:** Director/Designer	
Sales: 40.24M	**Franchise:** Mario	

Super Mario Bros. is a side-scrolling platformer comprised of eight worlds, and each world has four levels. The player must make Mario run, jump, throw fireballs, and solve spatial puzzles in order to save Princess Toadstool from the hands of Bowser. Miyamoto designed horizontal and vertical space (main land levels, sky levels, and sewer and swimming levels) as well as warp zones that would allow players to traverse the map quickly. This highly influential game came packaged, along with Duck Hunt, with the NES console. Luigi can only be played in two-player mode.

Super Mario Bros. 2	NA: 1989 JP: 1988 EU: 1992
Platform: Nintendo Entertainment System	**Role:** Producer/Designer
Sales: 7.46M	**Franchise:** Mario

Originally released for the Famicom Disk System in Japan in 1986, *Super Mario Bros. 2* continues iterating on many of the features of the first game. To the jump and fire play mechanics, the director and designers added more complex-level designs that require players to pick up and move objects, introduced new enemies, and developed weather features to this side-scrolling platformer. Players can take on four protagonist roles: Mario, Luigi, Princess Toadstool, and Toad (each with different character attributes) to save Subcon from Wart.

Super Mario Bros. 3	NA: 1990 JP: 1988 EU: 1991
Platform: Nintendo Entertainment System	**Role:** Director
Sales: 17.28M	**Franchise:** Mario

A side-scrolling platform game, this game introduces a number of new gameplay mechanics, including flying, turning into protective stone, and sliding quickly down slopes. Players can also now traverse the different worlds and levels using a world map, which becomes a staple of future Mario games. The simple story has Bowser's seven children, the Koopalings, ruling over each of the seven conquered kingdoms, with Bowser holding the final kingdom. Players must find the wand and save the kingdom. This game continues to appear on top video game lists and has spun off into an animated series as well.

Super Mario Galaxy	NA: 2007 JP: 2007 EU: 2007
Platform: Wii	**Role:** Producer/Designer
Sales: 11.09M	**Franchise:** Mario

Super Mario Galaxy takes the metaphor of "worlds" and extends it to small planetary systems in space. Again, Mario must defeat Bowser, moving among the different galaxies to collect Power Stars. The main gameplay mechanic manipulates a physics system that provides each planet and celestial sphere with its own gravitational pull. Players can manipulate that gravity to jump planet to planet, walk upside-down and sideways, and run around planets to surprise enemies from behind.

Mario Paint	NA: 1992 JP: 1992 EU: 1992
Platform: Super Nintendo Entertainment System	**Role:** Producer/Designer
Sales: 2.75M	**Franchise:** Mario

Packaged with a mouse and mouse pad, *Mario Paint* provides users/players with a basic drawing program that includes a palette of textures and patterns, stamps, and specialty erasers. In addition to this, people can build their own stamps pixel by pixel; they can create simple animations; and they can set animations to music generated by the program. While the main purpose of the game is a drawing program, included within is also a fly-swatting minigame.

Mario Artist: Paint Studio	NA: 0 JP: 1999 EU: 0
Platform: Nintendo 64DD	**Role:** Director/Supervisor
Sales: not available	**Franchise:** Mario

This is a return to *Mario Paint*, providing players with a drawing program that utilizes the processing power of the 64DD. Players can use a variety of brush sizes and textures to create colorful pictures. Further, like the previous iteration, this also includes both the ability to animate and play small minigames.

Super Mario Bros: The Lost Levels		NA: 0 JP: 1986 EU: 0
Platform: Famicom	**Role:** Producer	
Sales: 2.65M	**Franchise:** Mario	

Super Mario World		NA: 1991 JP: 1990 EU: 1992
Platform: Super Nintendo Entertainment System	**Role:** Producer	
Sales: 20.61M	**Franchise:** Mario	

Super Mario World 2: Yoshi's Island		NA: 1995 JP: 1995 EU: 1995
Platform: Super Nintendo Entertainment System	**Role:** Producer	
Sales: 4.12M	**Franchise:** Mario	

Super Mario All-Stars		NA: 1993 JP: 1993 EU: 1993
Platform: Super Nintendo Entertainment System	**Role:** Producer	
Sales: 10.55M	**Franchise:** Mario	

Super Mario 64		NA: 1996 JP: 1996 EU: 1997
Platform: Nintendo 64	**Role:** Producer	
Sales: 11.89M	**Franchise:** Mario	

BS Super Mario USA Power Challenge		NA: 0 JP: 1996 EU: 0
Platform: Super Famicom/ Stellaview	**Role:** Producer	
Sales: N/A	**Franchise:** Mario	

Super Mario RPG: Legend of the Seven Stars	NA: 1996 JP: 1996 EU: 0
Platform: Super Nintendo Entertainment System	**Role:** Producer
Sales: 2.14M	**Franchise:** Mario

Mario Party	NA: 1999 JP: 1998 EU: 1999
Platform: Nintendo 64	**Role:** Supervisor
Sales: 2.70M	**Franchise:** Mario

Mario Golf	NA: 1999 JP: 1999 EU: 1999
Platform: Nintendo 64	**Role:** Supervisor
Sales: 1.47M	**Franchise:** Mario

Mario Golf: Toadstool Tour	NA: 2003 JP: 2003 EU: 2004
Platform: GameCube	**Role:** Producer
Sales: 1.53M	**Franchise:** Mario

Mario Golf: World Tour	NA: 2014 JP: 2014 EU: 2014
Platform: 3DS	**Role:** Producer/Supervisor
Sales: 0.23M	**Franchise:** Mario

Paper Mario	NA: 2001 JP: 2000 EU: 2001
Platform: Nintendo 64	**Role:** Producer
Sales: 1.38M	**Franchise:** Mario

Paper Mario: The Thousand-Year Door	NA: 2004 JP: 2004 EU: 2004
Platform: GameCube	**Role:** Producer
Sales: 2.25M	**Franchise:** Mario

Super Paper Mario	NA: 2007 JP: 2007 EU: 2007
Platform: Wii	**Role:** Producer
Sales: 3.65M	**Franchise:** Mario

Super Mario Advance	NA: 2001 JP: 2001 EU: 2001
Platform: GBA	**Role:** Producer
Sales: 5.49M	**Franchise:** Mario

Luigi's Mansion	NA: 2001 JP: 2001 EU: 2002
Platform: GameCube	**Role:** Producer
Sales: 3.60M	**Franchise:** Mario

Super Mario World: Super Mario Advance 2	NA: 2002 JP: 2001 EU: 2002
Platform: GBA	**Role:** Producer
Sales: 5.46M	**Franchise:** Mario

Super Mario Sunshine	NA: 2002 JP: 2002 EU: 2002
Platform: GameCube	**Role:** Producer
Sales: 6.31M	**Franchise:** Mario

Mario & Luigi: Superstar Saga	NA: 2003 JP: 2003 EU: 2003
Platform: GBA	**Role:** Producer
Sales: 2.17M	**Franchise:** Mario

Super Mario 64 DS	NA: 2004 JP: 2004 EU: 2005
Platform: DS	**Role:** Producer/Supervising Director
Sales: 10.17M	**Franchise:** Mario

Mario vs. Donkey Kong 2: March of the Minis	NA: 2007 JP: 2006 EU: 2007
Platform: DS	**Role:** Producer
Sales: 1.18M	**Franchise:** Mario

Mario vs. Donkey Kong: Minis March Again!	NA: 2009 JP: 2009 EU: 2009
Platform: DSi	**Role:** Producer
Sales: N/A	**Franchise:** Mario

Mario & Sonic at the Olympic Games	NA: 2007 JP: 2007 EU: 2007
Platform: Wii	**Role:** Producer
Sales: 7.94M	**Franchise:** Mario

Super Mario Galaxy 2	NA: 2010 JP: 2010 EU: 2010
Platform: Wii	**Role:** Producer
Sales: 7.25M	**Franchise:** Mario

Super Mario 3D Land	NA: 2011 JP: 2011 EU: 2011
Platform: 3DS	**Role:** Producer
Sales: 9.58M	**Franchise:** Mario

New Super Mario Bros. U	NA: 2012 JP: 2012 EU: 2012
Platform: WiiU	**Role:** Producer
Sales: 4.18M	**Franchise:** Mario

Nintendo Land	NA: 2012 JP: 2012 EU: 2012
Platform: WiiU	**Role:** Producer
Sales: 3.10M	**Franchise:** Mario

Luigi's Mansion: Dark Moon	NA: 2013 JP: 2013 EU: 2013
Platform: 3DS	**Role:** Producer
Sales: 3.77M	**Franchise:** Mario

Super Mario 3D World	NA: 2013 JP: 2013 EU: 2013
Platform: WiiU	**Role:** Producer
Sales: 2.23M	**Franchise:** Mario

New Super Mario Bros.	NA: 2006 JP: 2006 EU: 2006
Platform: DS	**Role:** Supervisor
Sales: 29.49M	**Franchise:** Mario

New Super Mario Bros. Wii		NA: 2009 JP: 2009 EU: 2009
Platform: Wii	**Role:** Producer	
Sales: 27.50M	**Franchise:** Mario	

Mario Strikers Charged		NA: 2007 JP: 2007 EU: 2007
Platform: Wii	**Role:** Producer/Supervisor	
Sales: 2.54M	**Franchise:** Mario	

The Legend of Zelda

The Legend of Zelda		NA: 1986 JP: 1987 EU: 1987
Platform: Nintendo Entertainment System	**Role:** Director/Producer/ Designer	
Sales: 6.51M	**Franchise:** Zelda	

The Legend of Zelda is an adventure game in which the player must rescue Princess Zelda and the Triforce from the evil clutches of Ganon. The player must navigate an aboveground terrain—referred to as the overworld—to open secret doors, gather artifacts, and defeat enemies while also uncovering eight dungeons in the search for the missing Triforce pieces. Once the Triforce of Wisdom is reassembled, the player can enter the ninth dungeon to save Zelda. The map is comprised of varying environments, and enemies, friends, and objects are hidden throughout the map. The game cartridge came complete with an internal battery and memory storage so that players could save their progress and return to the game. Further, when players completed the game, they could return via a Second Quest in which objects are rearranged and monsters are more difficult to kill.

BS Zelda no Densetsu *(BS The Legend of Zelda)*	NA: 0 JP: 1995 EU: 0
Platform: Super Famicom/ Stellaview	**Role:** Designer
Sales: N/A	**Franchise:** Zelda

Released in Japan only, this game is merely an expansion of the first *Legend of Zelda* (sometimes referred to as the Third Quest). Players could download this game to their Satellaview extension, saving it to the base unit's memory or onto a special cassette. The overworld was altered slightly, dungeons were changed, and players could now collect up to 999 rupees.

The Legend of Zelda: Ocarina of Time	NA: 1998 JP: 1998 EU: 1998
Platform: Nintendo 64	**Role:** Director/Producer
Sales: 7.60M	**Franchise:** Zelda

This action-adventure game has enjoyed constant critical acclaim since its release. This is the first 3D Zelda game and one of the early releases for the Nintendo 64. Once again, it returns to Hyrule, and players start with a child Link but will be able to play as adult Link after finding the Master Sword. This game has both a more complicated plot and more sophisticated gameplay mechanisms, such as Z-targeting, which introduces context-sensitive actions in combat. Players must use weapons and objects to defeat monsters, and the player is sometimes called upon to use stealth. The game includes traditional puzzles as well as musical challenges: players must learn to play certain songs on the ocarina, incorporating music into the game as active action. In addition to the main quest, player can opt into a series of side quests.

Zelda II: The Adventure of Link	NA: 1987 JP: 1987 EU: 1988
Platform: Nintendo Entertainment System	**Role:** Producer
Sales: 4.38M	**Franchise:** Zelda

The Legend of Zelda: A Link to the Past	NA: 1991 JP: 1992 EU: 1992
Platform: Super Nintendo Entertainment System	**Role:** Producer
Sales: 4.61M	**Franchise:** Zelda

The Legend of Zelda: Link's Awakening	NA: 1993 JP: 1993 EU: 1993
Platform: GB	**Role:** Producer
Sales: 3.83M	**Franchise:** Zelda

The Legend of Zelda: Majora's Mask	NA: 2000 JP: 2000 EU: 2000
Platform: Nintendo 64	**Role:** Producer
Sales: 3.36M	**Franchise:** Zelda

The Legend of Zelda: Oracle of Seasons	NA: 2001 JP: 2001 EU: 2001
Platform: GBC	**Role:** Producer
Sales: 1.86M	**Franchise:** Zelda

The Legend of Zelda: Oracle of Ages	NA: 2001 JP: 2001 EU: 2001
Platform: GBC	**Role:** Producer
Sales: 1.92M	**Franchise:** Zelda

The Legend of Zelda: The Wind Waker	NA: 2003 JP: 2002 EU: 2003
Platform: GameCube	**Role:** Producer
Sales: 4.60M	**Franchise:** Zelda

The Legend of Zelda: *Four Swords Adventures*	NA: 2004 JP: 2004 EU: 2005
Platform: GameCube	**Role:** Producer
Sales: 0.81M	**Franchise:** Zelda

The Legend of Zelda: The Minish Cap	NA: 2004 JP: 2004 EU: 2005
Platform: GBA	**Role:** Producer
Sales: 1.42M	**Franchise:** Zelda

The Legend of Zelda: Twilight Princess	NA: 2006 JP: 2006 EU: 2006
Platform: GameCube/Wii	**Role:** Producer
Sales: 8.56M	**Franchise:** Zelda

The Legend of Zelda: Phantom Hourglass	NA: 2007 JP: 2007 EU: 2007
Platform: DS	**Role:** Producer
Sales: 5.02M	**Franchise:** Zelda

Link's Crossbow Training	NA: 2008 JP: 2007 EU: 2007
Platform: Wii	**Role:** Producer
Sales: 4.95M	**Franchise:** Zelda

The Legend of Zelda: Skyward Sword	NA: 2011 JP: 2011 EU: 2011
Platform: Wii	**Role:** Producer
Sales: 3.77M	**Franchise:** Zelda

The Legend of Zelda: Ocarina of Time 3D	NA: 2011 JP: 2011 EU: 2011
Platform: 3DS	**Role:** Producer
Sales: 3.39M	**Franchise:** Zelda

The Legend of Zelda: The Wind Waker HD	NA: 2013 JP: 2013 EU: 2013
Platform: WiiU	**Role:** Producer
Sales: 1.04M	**Franchise:** Zelda

Mario Kart

Super Mario Kart	NA: 1992 JP: 1992 EU: 1993
Platform: Super Nintendo Entertainment System	**Role:** Producer
Sales: 8.76M	**Franchise:** Mario Kart

This is a go-cart style racing game with two single-player modes (Grand Prix and Time Trial) and three multiplayer modes (Mario Kart Grand Prix, Match Race, and Battle Mode). Grand Prix, or GP, modes are simple races; and in multiplayer mode, two players can play simultaneously on a split screen. Match Race allows two players to race without any computer opponents, and the Battle Mode provides each player with three balloons that other characters are attempting to pop—a notable mechanic different from the timing-based win conditions of racing games. There are eight playable characters from the Mario and Donkey Kong universes, and players can collect power-ups, such as slippery banana peels and Koopa shells to lay traps for one another.

Mario Kart 64		NA: 1996 JP: 1997 EU: 1997
Platform: Nintendo 64	**Role:** Producer	
Sales: 9.87M	**Franchise:** Mario Kart	

Mario Kart: Super Circuit		NA: 2001 JP: 2001 EU: 2001
Platform: GBA	**Role:** Producer	
Sales: 5.47M	**Franchise:** Mario Kart	

Mario Kart: Double Dash		NA: 2003 JP: 2003 EU: 2003
Platform: GameCube	**Role:** Producer	
Sales: 6.95M	**Franchise:** Mario Kart	

Mario Kart DS		NA: 2005 JP: 2005 EU: 2005
Platform: DS	**Role:** Producer	
Sales: 22.93M	**Franchise:** Mario Kart	

Mario Kart Wii		NA: 2008 JP: 2008 EU: 2008
Platform: Wii	**Role:** Producer	
Sales: 34.61M	**Franchise:** Mario Kart	

Mario Kart 7		NA: 2011 JP: 2011 EU: 2011
Platform: 3DS	**Role:** Producer	
Sales: 9.78M	**Franchise:** Mario Kart	

Mario Kart 8	NA: 2014 JP: 2014 EU: 2014
Platform: WiiU	**Role:** Producer
Sales: 2.58M	**Franchise:** Mario Kart

Smash Bros.

Super Smash Bros.	NA: 1999 JP: 1999 EU: 1999
Platform: Nintendo 64	**Role:** Producer
Sales: 5.55M	**Franchise:** Smash Bros.

Super Smash Bros. represents Nintendo's take on a fighting game in which players compete to knock each other out of a platform stage. Players can fight as characters from various Nintendo franchises, including Mario, Zelda, Pokémon, Kirby, and Metroid; each with their own set of fighting moves. Unlike other fighting games, *Super Smash Bros.* does not rely on long button combinations or fixed character positions but instead defines attacks based on a single button and control stick position and allows players to move freely about the arena. During the fight, random Nintendo-themed item drops such as shells and Pokeballs provide weapons and power-ups for dealing additional damage and health recovery. The game provides both single-player modes, in which players complete in timed tournaments, and up to four-player multiplayer with configurable game rules. Since its initial release on the N64, the game has spawned a series of titles with similar gameplay mechanics on all following platforms.

Super Smash Bros.: Melee	NA: 2001 JP: 2001 EU: 2002
Platform: GameCube	**Role:** Producer
Sales: 7.07M	**Franchise:** Smash Bros.

Super Smash Bros.: Brawl		NA: 2008 JP: 2008 EU: 2008
Platform: Wii	**Role:** Producer	
Sales: 12.24M	**Franchise:** Smash Bros.	

Kirby

Kirby's Adventure		NA: 1993 JP: 1993 EU: 1993
Platform: NES	**Role:** Producer	
Sales: 1.75M	**Franchise:** Kirby	

Kirby Super Star		NA: 1996 JP: 1996 EU: 1996
Platform: Super Nintendo Entertainment System	**Role:** Producer	
Sales: 1.44M	**Franchise:** Kirby	

Kirby 64: The Crystal Shards		NA: 2000 JP: 2000 EU: 2001
Platform: Nintendo 64	**Role:** Supervisor	
Sales: 1.77M	**Franchise:** Kirby	

Kirby Air Ride		NA: 2003 JP: 2003 EU: 2004
Platform: GameCube	**Role:** Producer	
Sales: 1.62M	**Franchise:** Kirby	

Star Fox

Star Fox		NA: 1993 JP: 1993 EU: 1993
Platform: Super Nintendo Entertainment System	**Role:** Designer/Producer	

Sales: 2.99M	Franchise: Star Fox

Star Fox is an early example of a 3D rail shooter that asks the player to fly Arwings, a special type of spacecraft, through a series of courses that are populated by enemy fighters. Each player receives a wingman, whom the player can choose to help or ignore when asked (ignoring requests for help will likely result in the wingman sustaining damage or getting shot down). There are three unique routes that the player can take, corresponding with difficulty levels. Arwings have the ability to use their thrusters to speed up or retro-rockets to slow down, and they are protected by an energy shield that will alleviate some damage.

Star Fox 64		NA: 1997 JP: 1997 EU: 1997
Platform: Nintendo 64	Role: Producer	
Sales: 4.03M	Franchise: Star Fox	

Star Fox 64 3D		NA: 2011 JP: 2011 EU: 2011
Platform: 3DS	Role: Producer	
Sales: 0.81M	Franchise: Star Fox	

Star Fox Adventures		NA: 2002 JP: 2002 EU: 2002
Platform: GameCube	Role: Producer	
Sales: 1.87M	Franchise: Star Fox	

Star Fox: Assault		NA: 2005 JP: 2005 EU: 2005
Platform: GameCube	Role: Producer	
Sales: 1.08M	Franchise: Star Fox	

Pikmin

Pikmin	NA: 2001 JP: 2001 EU: 2002
Platform: GameCube	**Role:** Producer/Concept Creator
Sales: 1.63M	**Franchise:** Pikmin

Based on Miyamoto's gardening hobby, *Pikmin* is a simple strategy game in which the player plays as Olimar, a space alien who crash lands on a foreign planet. Olimar must gather the missing parts of his spaceship, and for that, he finds and collects red, yellow, and blue pikmin—small plant creatures that follow Olimar's directions. Olimar, in return, must care for these little creatures, calling them back every night to protect them from predators. The player controls Olimar, and Olimar controls the pikmin. The pikmin collaborate to carry objects, scout, break walls, and attack enemies.

Pikmin 2	NA: 2004 JP: 2004 EU: 2004
Platform: GameCube	**Role:** Producer
Sales: 1.20M	**Franchise:** Pikmin

Pikmin 3	NA: 2013 JP: 2013 EU: 2013
Platform: WiiU	**Role:** Producer
Sales: 0.80M	**Franchise:** Pikmin

Animal Crossing

Animal Crossing	NA: 2002 JP: 2001 EU: 2004
Platform: GameCube	**Role:** Supervisor
Sales: 3.15M	**Franchise:** Animal Crossing

Animal Crossing is a simulation game in which players start as a person in a village, talking with other animals who live there, performing small tasks, fishing, and collecting items. The game is played in real time by utilizing the internal clock and calendar. Further, players are allowed a high degree of customization, affecting both the avatars' looks and the houses that the player creates and furnishes. At heart, this is a community-based game focused on individual expression and care.

Metroid

Metroid Prime	NA: 2002 JP: 2003 EU: 2003
Platform: GameCube	**Role:** Producer
Sales: 2.82M	**Franchise:** Metroid

Nintendogs

Nintendogs	NA: 2005 JP: 2005 EU: 2005
Platform: DS	**Role:** Producer/Concept Creator
Sales: 24.60M	**Franchise:** Nintendogs

Nintendogs is a pet simulation game in which players take care of their electronic dogs. This uses the touch screen and the microphone to allow players to have more immediate correlations between input and action—players can "pet" their dog with the touch screen or blow bubbles by blowing into the microphone. In addition to walking pets and playing with them, players can also enter their pets into competitions, which will earn them in-game currency, which in turn allows the player to purchase things for their dogs. Finally, this game uses the DS's wireless networking capabilities to allow two people with unique Nintendogs together, and let those dogs play together on the same screen.

Nintendogs + Cats	NA: 2011 JP: 2011 EU: 2011
Platform: 3DS	**Role:** Producer
Sales: 3.38M	**Franchise:** Nintendogs

Pokémon

Pokémon Red and Blue	NA: 1998 JP: 1996 EU: 1999
Platform: GB	**Role:** Producer
Sales: 31.37M	**Franchise:** Pokémon

Pokémon Stadium	NA: 2000 JP: 1999 EU: 2000
Platform: Nintendo 64	**Role:** Producer
Sales: 5.45M	**Franchise:** Pokémon

Wii

Wii Sports	NA: 2006 JP: 2006 EU: 2006
Platform: Wii	**Role:** Producer
Sales: 82.07M	**Franchise:** Wii

Wii Sports includes a set of sports games designed to demonstrate the motion capabilities of the Wii Remote. In each game, players use the Wii Remote to simulate actions of players in real-life sports, including tennis, baseball, bowling, golf, and boxing. For example, players can hold the Wii Remote like a golf club and swing it in a manner similar to a real golf player. Packaged with every Wii console, the game provides a way to introduce users to the Wii motion controls. Each game includes a training mode to allow players to practice with the controller and game mechanic, for which players are rewarded with medals based on their progress. In addition, multiplayer modes for each game allow players to face each other—represented by their Mii characters—for skill points recorded to their profile.

Wii Music	NA: 2008 JP: 2008 EU: 2008
Platform: Wii	**Role:** Producer/Designer
Sales: 3.22M	**Franchise:** Wii

Inspired by Miyamoto's love of music, *Wii Music* allows players to arrange their own musical compositions by controlling an on-screen band. Unlike other music games that involve playing a song correctly, *Wii Music* encourages original compositions and experimentation. The game includes sixty-six playable instruments, which range from traditional strings, percussion, and winds, to various vocals, shouts, cat and dog sounds, and an "NES Horn" that features the familiar synthesized sounds produced by the 8-bit console. Players can manipulate the instruments by selecting a group of instruments with the Wii Remote's motion controls—for example, holding the Wii Remote like a trumpet—and playing specific notes with the buttons. In "Jam Mode," one or more players can play a predefined song with a specific instrument for each player. While playing, the game does not view specific player inputs as "correct," but instead tries to make each button press sound harmonious with the music (Kohler 2008).

Wii Fit	NA: 2008 JP: 2007 EU: 2008
Platform: Wii	**Role:** Producer
Sales: 22.69M	**Franchise:** Wii

Inspired by Miyamoto's desire to exercise and keep track of his weight, *Wii Fit* provides a set of activities to facilitate players' exercise habits. The game was bundled with the Wii Balance Board peripheral, which looks similar to a bathroom scale and contains sensors for measuring a player's weight and center of balance. Using this device, players can track their weight and participate in a number of exercise-related games including yoga, strength training, and aerobics. The games are scored based on the player's ability to maintain their center of balance as defined by the activity. Players can track their weight and progress in the activities through a profile connected to their

Mii characters, many of which can be stored on the same console. Miyamoto targeted this game toward family use, envisioning parents and their children each using the system to track their exercise habits.

Punch-Out!!	NA: 2007 JP: 2007 EU: 2007
Platform: Wii	**Role:** Supervisor
Sales: 0.25M	**Franchise:** Wii

Yoshi

Yoshi	NA: 1991 JP: 1991 EU: 1992
Platform: Nintendo Entertainment System	**Role:** Producer
Sales: 1.75M	**Franchise:** Yoshi

Yoshi's Safari	NA: 1993 JP: 1993 EU: 1993
Platform: Super Nintendo Entertainment System	**Role:** Producer
Sales: N/A	**Franchise:** Yoshi

Yoshi's Island: Super Mario Advance 3	NA: 2002 JP: 2002 EU: 2002
Platform: GBA	**Role:** Producer
Sales: 2.91M	**Franchise:** Yoshi

Yoshi's Story	NA: 1997 JP: 1998 EU: 1998
Platform: Nintendo 64	**Role:** Supervisor
Sales: 2.85M	**Franchise:** Yoshi

Additional Games in Alphabetical Order

1080° TenEighty Snowboarding	NA: 1998 JP: 1998 EU: 1998
Platform: Nintendo 64	**Role:** Producer
Sales: 2.03M	**Franchise:** 1080°

1080° Avalanche	NA: 2003 JP: 2003 EU: 2004
Platform: GameCube	**Role:** Producer
Sales: N/A	**Franchise:** 1080°

Chibi-Robo! Plug Into Adventure!	NA: 2005 JP: 2005 EU: 2006
Platform: GameCube	**Role:** Producer
Sales: 0.39M	**Franchise:** Chibi-Robo

Disney's Magical Mirror Starring Mickey Mouse	NA: 2002 JP: 2002 EU: 2002
Platform: GameCube	**Role:** Producer
Sales: 0.19M	**Franchise:** Disney

Doshin the Giant	NA: 0 JP: 2002 EU: 2002
Platform: GameCube	**Role:** Producer
Sales: 0.14M	**Franchise:** Doshin

Eternal Darkness: Sanity's Requiem	NA: 2002 JP: 2002 EU: 2002
Platform: GameCube	**Role:** Producer
Sales: 0.44M	**Franchise:** N/A

F-Zero	NA: 1991 JP: 1990 EU: 1992
Platform: Super Nintendo Entertainment System	**Role:** Producer
Sales: 2.85M	**Franchise:** F-Zero

F-Zero X	NA: 1998 JP: 1998 EU: 1998
Platform: Nintendo 64	**Role:** Producer
Sales: 1.10M	**Franchise:** F-Zero

F-Zero GX	NA: 2003 JP: 2003 EU: 2003
Platform: GameCube	**Role:** Producer
Sales: 0.65M	**Franchise:** F-Zero

Geist	NA: 2005 JP: 0 EU: 2005
Platform: GameCube	**Role:** Producer
Sales: 0.15M	**Franchise:** Geist

GiFTPiA	NA: 0 JP: 2003 EU: 0
Platform: GameCube	**Role:** Producer
Sales: 0.11M	**Franchise:**

Hamtaro: Ham-Ham Heartbreak	NA: 2003 JP: 2002 EU: 2003
Platform: GBA	**Role:** Producer
Sales: 0.36M	**Franchise:** Hamtaro

Hamtaro: Rainbow Rescue	NA: 2004 JP: 2003 EU: 0
Platform: GBA	**Role:** Producer
Sales: N/A	**Franchise:** Hamtaro

Ice Climber	NA: 1985 JP: 1985 EU: 1986
Platform: Nintendo Entertainment System	**Role:** Producer
Sales: 1.50M	**Franchise:** N/A

Kid Icarus	NA: 1987 JP: 1986 EU: 1987
Platform: Nintendo Entertainment System	**Role:** Producer
Sales: 1.76M	**Franchise:** Kid Icarus

Mole Mania	NA: 1997 JP: 1996 EU: 1997
Platform: GB	**Role:** Producer
Sales: N/A	**Franchise:**

Mother	NA: 0 JP: 1989 EU: 0
Platform: Famicom	**Role:** Producer
Sales: 0.4M	**Franchise:** Mother

Pac-Man vs.	NA: 2003 JP: 0 EU: 2004
Platform: GameCube	**Role:** Director
Sales: N/A	**Franchise:** Pac-Man

Pilotwings	NA: 1991 JP: 1990 EU: 1993
Platform: Super Nintendo Entertainment System	**Role:** Producer
Sales: 1.14M	**Franchise:** Pilotwings

Pilotwings 64	NA: 1996 JP: 1996 EU: 1997
Platform: Nintendo 64	**Role:** Producer
Sales: 1.12M	**Franchise:** Pilotwings

Steel Diver	NA: 2011 JP: 2011 EU: 2011
Platform: 3DS	**Role:** Producer
Sales: 0.42M	**Franchise:** Steel Diver

Stunt Race FX	NA: 1994 JP: 1994 EU: 1994
Platform: Super Nintendo Entertainment System	**Role:** Producer
Sales: 0.35M	**Franchise:**

Wave Race	NA: 1992 JP: 0 EU: 1997
Platform: GB	**Role:** Producer
Sales: N/A	**Franchise:** Wave Race

Wave Race 64		NA: 1996 JP: 1996 EU: 1997
Platform: Nintendo 64	**Role:** Producer	
Sales: 2.94M	**Franchise:** Wave Race	

Wave Race: Blue Storm		NA: 2001 JP: 2001 EU: 2002
Platform: GameCube	**Role:** Producer	
Sales: 0.60M	**Franchise:** Wave Race	

Works Cited

"A First-rate Link, Even by Nintendo Standards." n.d. *Iwata Asks: The Legend of Zelda: Twilight Princess.* http://iwataasks.nintendo.com/interviews/#/wii/twilight_princess/0/7

"A Life-Changing Game." n.d. *Iwata Asks: A Life-changing Game.* Accessed August 1, 2014. http://iwataasks.nintendo.com/interviews/#/ds/diy/0/4

"A Mario Even Beginners Can Play." n.d. *Iwata Asks: Super Mario Galaxy.* http://iwataasks.nintendo.com/interviews/#/wii/super_mario_galaxy/0/2

"A Truly Ground breaking Collection of Games." n.d. *Iwata Asks: Wii Sports.* http://iwataasks.nintendo.com/interviews/#/wii/wii_sports/0/0

"A Wondrous Experience." n.d. *Iwata Asks: Nintendo 3DS Guides: Louvre.* http://iwataasks.nintendo.com/interviews/#/3ds/louvre-guide/0/3

"Adjusting the Map in a Daily Cycle." n.d. *Iwata Asks: New Super Mario Bros.* Accessed August 1, 2014. http://iwataasks.nintendo.com/interviews/#/wii/nsmb/1/4

Adventure. 1979. Atari. Video Game.

Alvzrez, Louis and Andy Kolker. 1991. *The Japanese Version,* DVD. New York: Center for New American Media.

Ama, Toshimaro. 2005. *Why are the Japanese Non-Religious?: Japanese Spirituality: Being Non-Religious in a Religious Culture.* Lanham, MD: University Press of America.

Angry Birds Space. 2012. Robio. Video Game.

Animal Crossing (US) / *Animal Forest* (JP). 2002. Nintendo. Video Game.

Asteroids. 1979. Atari. Video Game.

Ball. 1980. Nintendo. Video Game.

Baranowski, Tom, Dina Abdelsamad, Janice Baranowski, Teresia Margareta O'Connor, Debbe Thompson, Anthony Barnett, Ester Cerin, and Tzu-An Chen. 2012. "Impact of an Active Video Game on Healthy Children's Physical Activity." *Journal of the American Academy of Pediatrics* 93.8: 1084–91.

Baratto, Giorgio. 2002. "Interview to Shigeru Miyamoto, the 'mother' of Mario." *Videogame.it,* February 18. http://www.videogame.it/shigeru-miyamoto-inglese-pc/1991/interview-to-shigeru-miyamoto-the-mother-of-mario.html

Barthes, Roland. 1967, Translation 1977. "Death of an Author." In *Image / Music / Text*, translated by Stephen Heath, 142–47. New York: Hill and Wang.

Bogost, Ian. 2008. "The Rhetoric of Video Games." In *The Ecology of Games: Connecting Youth, Games, and Learning*, edited by Katie Salen. The John D. and Catherine T. MacArthur Foundation Series on Digital Media and Learning, 117–40. Cambridge, MA: The MIT Press.

Bolman, Lee G. and Terrence E. Deal. 2008. *Reframing Organizations: Artistry, Choice and Leadership*, 4th ed. San Francisco, CA: John Wiley & Sons.

"Bonus Stage 1: Ancient Documents from 1985." n.d. *Iwata Asks: Nintendo DS*. Accessed July 1, 2014. http://iwataasks.nintendo.com/interviews/#/ds/zelda/1/4

Brown, Scott and Michelle Kung. 2008. "The 2008 TIME 100 Finalists." *TIME Magazine*. http://content.time.com/time/specials/2007/article/0,28804,1725112_1726934_1726935,00.html

Caillois, Roger. 1961. *Man, Play, and Games*. Paris: The Free Press/Simon and Schuster.

Call of Duty. 2003. Infinity Ward. Video Game.

Campbell, Joseph. 2008. *The Hero with a Thousand Faces*, 3rd ed. Novato, CA: New World Library.

Clark, K. B. and T. Fujimoto. *Product Development Performance: Strategy, Organization, and Management in the World Auto Industry*. Boston, MA: Harvard Business School Press.

Cook, Dave. 2013. "Miyamoto Discusses the Role of Females in Game Narratives." *VG247*, June 21. http://www.vg247.com/2013/06/21/miyamoto-discussed-the-role-of-females-in-game-narratives/

Costikyan, Greg. 2013. *Uncertainty in Games*. Playful Thinking. Cambridge, MA: The MIT Press.

"Counselor's Corner." 1988. *Nintendo Power*, September/October, 66–67.

Crash Bandicoot. Naughty Dog. 1996. Video Game.

Crecente, Brian. 2011. "How one coin saved arcades in Japan and another killed them in the U.S." *Kotaku*, February 22. http://kotaku.com/5767303/how-one-coin-saved-arcades-in-japan-and-killed-them-in-the-us

Crecente, Brian. June 16, 2014, 12:00pm. Twitter post, "Mario's creator is fighting for the heart of the Wii U, but it might be too late." http://twitter.com/crecenteb

Crigger, Lara. 2007. "Searching for Gunpei Yokoi." *The Escapist*, March 6. http://www.escapistmagazine.com/articles/view/video-games/issues/ issue_87/490-Searching-for-Gunpei-Yokoi

Cross, Nigel. 2008. *Engineering Design Methods: Strategies for Product Design.* West Sussex, UK: Wiley.

Curry, Patrick. 2009. "Everything I Know About Game Design I Learned from Super Mario Bros." In *Well Played 1.0: Video Games, Value, and Meaning,* edited by Drew Davidson, 7–19. Pittsburgh, PA: ETC Press.

Cyto. 2014. Room 8. Video Game.

D'Angelo, William. "2014 Year on Year Sales and Market Share Update to August 9th." *VGChartz*, August 20. http://www.vgchartz.com/ article/251787/2014-year-on-year-sales-and-market-share-update-to- august-9th/

Darrell, Larry. 2014. "The 5 Most Influential Video-Game Designers." *Bidness Etc*, May 31. http://www.bidnessetc.com/business/the-most-5-influential- video-game-designers/

de Certeau, Michel. 1984. *The Practice of Everyday Life.* Berkeley: University of California Press.

"Deeper and Wider." n.d. *Iwata Asks: E3 2011: Wii U.* http://iwataasks. nintendo.com/interviews/#/e32011/newhw/0/6

deWinter, J. 2009. "Aesthetic Reproduction in Japanese Computer Culture: The Dialectical Histories of Manga, Anime, and Computer Games." In *Computer Culture Reader*, edited by Judd. E. Ruggill, Ken. S. McAllister, and Joseph. R. Chaney, 108–24. Cambridge, MA: Cambridge Scholar's Press.

"Did Anyone Say It Should Look Realistic?" n.d. *Iwata Asks: Wii Sports.* http://iwataasks.nintendo.com/interviews/#/wii/wii_sports/0/1

Doi, Takeo. 1973. *The Anatomy of Dependence.* Tokyo: Kodansha International.

Donkey Kong. Nintendo. 1981. Video Game.

Donovan, T. 2010. *Replay: The History of Videogames.* East Sussex, UK: Yellow Ant.

Drake, Audrey. 2012. "Nintendo Land Review." *IGN*, November 15. http:// www.ign.com/articles/2012/11/15/nintendo-land-review

Dymek, Mikolaj. 2010. "Industrial Phantasmagoria: Subcultural Interactive Cinema Meets Mass-Cultural Media of Simulation." PhD thesis in Industrial Economics and Management, Royal Institute of Technology Stockholm, Sweden.

"E3 2004: Miyamoto and Aonuma on Zelda." 2004. *IGN*, May 12. http://www. ign.com/articles/2004/05/13/e3-2004-miyamoto-and-aonuma-on-zelda

Edge. 2014. "Retrospective: The Legend of Zelda: Ocarina of Time." *Edge Online*. http://www.edge-online.com/features/retrospective-the-legend-of-zelda-ocarina-of-time/

Ehrenreich, Barbara. 2006. *Dancing in the Streets: A History of Collective Joy*. New York: Metropolitan Books.

ESA Canada. 2013. "2013 Essential Facts about the Canadian Video Game Industry." Entertainment Software Association of Canada. http://theesa.ca/wp-content/uploads/2013/10/Essential-Facts-English.pdf

"Everyone Loves Horses." n.d. *Iwata Asks: The Legend of Zelda: Ocarina of Time 3D*. Accessed August 1, 2014. http://iwataasks.nintendo.com/interviews/#/3ds/zelda-ocarina-of-time/4/2

Excitebike. 1984. Nintendo. Video Game.

Farmville. 2009. Zynga. Video Game.

Fielder, Lauren. 1999. *Behind Zelda*. TechTV. January 8. http://www.techtv.com/extendedplay/videofeatures/story/0,24330,2185068,00.html

Fitzpatrick, Michael. 2013. "Can Japan Reboot its Anti-innovation Start-up Culture?" *BBC Future*, August 21.

Flutter. 2013. Runawayplay. Video Game.

"Focusing on the Player's Perspective." n.d. *Iwata Asks: The Legend of Zelda: Twilight Princess*. http://iwataasks.nintendo.com/interviews/#/wii/twilight_princess/0/6

Frasca, Gonzalo. 1999. "Ludology Meets Narratology: Similitude and differences between (video)games and narrative." *Ludology.com*.

Frasca, Gonzalo. 2003. "Simulating vs. Narrative: Introduction to Ludology." In *The Video Game Theory Reader*, edited by Mark Wolf and Bernard Perron, 221–35. New York: Routledge.

GamesRadar. 2010. "Gaming's Most Important Evolutions." *GamesRadar US*, October 8. http://www.gamesradar.com/gamings-most-important-evolutions

Gaudiosi, John. 2005. "Next Generation Game Concepts." *BusinessWeek*, November 30. http://www.businessweek.com/stories/2005-11-30/next-generation-game-concepts

Gestalt. 2001. "Pikmin Preview." *Eurogamer*, September 10. http://www.eurogamer.net/articles/p_pikmin

Gordon, Seth. 2007. *The King of Kong: A Fistful of Quarters*. New York: Picturehouse.

Grand Theft Auto: San Andreas. 2004. Rockstar Games. Video Game.

Grimm, Steven. 2005. "Link in a New Light: The Zelda Series Goes Where No Link Has Dared: Older, Darker and Much Hairier." *Nintendo Power* 193: 53–63.

Guide: Louvre. 2013. Nintendo. Audiovisual Guide for Nintendo 3DS.

Guitar Hero. 2005. Harmonix. Video Game.

Gulick, Luther Halsey. 1911. *The Healthful Art of Dancing.* New York: Doubleday, Page & Company.

Hall, Kenji. 2006. "The Big Ideas Behind Nintendo's Wii." *BusinessWeek*, November 16. Accessed via the Internet archive, https://web.archive.org/ web/20100207214825/http://www.businessweek.com/technology/content/ nov2006/tc20061116_750580.htm

Herbig, Paul and Laurence Jacobs. 1997. "A Historical Perspective of Japanese Innovation." *Management Decision* 35.10: 760–78. ProQuest. Accessed August 1, 2014.

"Hideki Konno." 2005. *Nintendo Power*, August 2005, vol. 194, 37.

"How Super Mario Was Born." n.d. *Iwata Asks: Super Mario Galaxy.* http:// iwataasks.nintendo.com/interviews/#/wii/super_mario_galaxy/0/0

Huizinga, Johan. 1955. *Homo Ludens: A Study of the Play-Element in Culture.* Boston, MA: Beacon Press.

Hutcheon, Linda. 2006. *A Theory of Adaptation.* New York: Routledge.

"Ideas Born Out of Functionality." n.d. *Iwata Asks: The Legend of Zelda: Twilight Princess.* http://iwataasks.nintendo.com/interviews/#/wii/ twilight_princess/0/1

IGN Staff. 1997. "Miyamoto Reveals Secrets: Fire Emblem, Mario Paint 64." *IGN*, July 29. http://www.ign.com/articles/1997/07/30/miyamoto-reveals-secrets-fire-emblem-mario-paint-64

Ikeya, Hayato. 2009. "僕らが作っているのは「作品」ではなく「商品」——宮本茂氏が 30年の仕事史を振り返る," "We Make Products and Not Works of Art—Shigeru Miyamoto Reflects on Thirty Years of Work." *IT Media Gamez*, October 27. Accessed July 16, 2014. http://gamez. itmedia.co.jp/games/articles/0910/27/news082.html

"Interview: CVG May 25th, 2002." 2002. Originally published by *Computer and Video Games* [CVG]. Archived by *ZeldaDungeon.net.* Accessed September 1, 2014. http://www.zeldadungeon.net/wiki/Interview:CVG_ May_25th_2002

"Interview: Famitsu October 27th 2001." 2001. Originally published by *Famitsu.* Archived by *ZeldaDungeon.net.* Accessed September 1, 2014.

http://www.zeldadungeon.net/wiki/Interview:Famitsu_
October_27th_2001

"Interview: GamePro April 1st, 2002." 2002. Originally published by *GamePro*. Archived by *ZeldaDungeon.net*. Accessed September 1, 2014. http://www. zeldadungeon.net/wiki/Interview:Famitsu_October_27th_2001

"Interview: Games Radar September 3rd 2000." 2000. *ZeldaDungeon. net*. Transcript of interview by Games Radar. Accessed September 1, 2014. http://www.zeldadungeon.net/wiki/Interview:Games_Radar_ September_3rd_2000

"Interview: Nintendo Online Magazine." 1998. Archived on ZeldaDungeon. net. August 1. http://www.zeldadungeon.net/wiki/Interview:Nintendo_ Online_Magazine_August_1st_1998

"Interview: Nintendo Power January 1998." 1998. Originally published by *Nintendo Power Source*. Archived by *ZeldaDungeon.net*. Accessed September 1, 2014. http://www.zeldadungeon.net/wiki/ Interview:Nintendo_Power_January_1998

"Interview: Shigeru Miyamoto and Satoru Iwata." 2002. *IGN*, March 4. http:// www.ign.com/articles/2002/03/04/interview-shigeru-miyamoto-and-satoru-iwata

"Interview: The 64 Dream April 22nd 1998." 1998. Originally published by *The 64 Dream*. Archived by *ZeldaDungeon.net*. Accessed September 1, 2014. http://www.zeldadungeon.net/wiki/Interview:The_64_Dream_ April_22nd_1998

"Interview: Time Digital 23rd April 1999." 1999. Originally published by *TIME Digital*. Archived by *ZeldaDungeon.net*. Accessed September 1, 2014. http:// www.zeldadungeon.net/wiki/Interview:Time_Digital_April_23rd_1999

"Interview: Tokyo University Lecture July 3rd 2003." 2003. Archived by *ZeldaDungeon.net*. Accessed September 1, 2014. http://www.zeldadungeon. net/wiki/Interview:Tokyo_University_Lecture_July_3rd_2003

"Introduction." n.d. *Iwata Asks: Wii Fit*. http://iwataasks.nintendo.com/ interviews/#/wii/wii_fit/0/0

Iszushi, Hiro and Yuko Aoyama. 2004. "Industry evolution and cross-sectoral skill transfers: a comparative analysis of the video game industry in Japan, the United States, and the United Kingdom." *Environment and Planning* 38.10: 1843–61.

"It Started with a Guy in Overalls." n.d. *Iwata Asks: Mario Kart Wii*. Accessed August 1, 2014. http://iwataasks.nintendo.com/interviews/#/wii/mariokart/0/0

"It Started with a Square Object Moving." n.d. *Iwata Asks: New Super Mario Bros.* Accessed August 1, 2014. http://iwataasks.nintendo.com/ interviews/#/wii/nsmb/1/3

Ivan, Tom. 2009. "Guinness Ranks Top 50 Games of All Time." Computer and Videogames.com. http://www.computerandvideogames.com/209385/ guinness-ranks-top-50-games-of-all-time/

Jenkins, Henry. 1998. "'Complete Freedom of Movement': Video Games as Gendered Play Spaces." In *From Barbie to Mortal Kombat: Gender and Computer Games*, edited by Justine Cassell and Henry Jenkins, 262–97. Cambridge, MA: The MIT Press.

Jenkins, Henry and Kurt Squire. 2002. "The Art of Contested Spaces." In *Game On!*, edited by Laurence King, 64–75. London: Barbican.

Jensen, Graham H. 2013. "Making Sense of Play in Video Games: *Ludus, Pradia*, and Possibility Spaces." *Eludamos. Journal for Computer Game Culture* 7.1: 69–80.

Jones, Darran. 2011. "Super Mario Kart: The Complete History of Nintendo's Kart Racer." *NowGamer*, November 28. http://www.nowgamer.com/ features/1148204/super_mario_kart_the_complete_history_of_ nintendos_kart_racer.html

Jones, Steven and George Thiruvathukal. 2012. *Codename Revolution: The Nintendo Wii Platform*. Cambridge, MA: The MIT Press.

Juul, Jesper. 2005. *Half-real: Video Games Between Real Rules and Fictional Worlds*. Cambridge, MA: The MIT Press.

Juul, Jesper. 2010. *A Casual Revolution: Reinventing Video Games and Their Players*. Cambridge, MA: The MIT Press.

Kaining, Kristin. 2007. "Sure, it's a cool job. But do games pay?" *NBC News*, On The Level, May 2. http://www.nbcnews.com/id/18406129/ns/ technology_and_science-games/t/sure-its-cool-job-do-games-pay/

Kaluszka, Aaron. 2007. "Eiki Aounuma's GDC 2007 Presentation." *Nintendo World Report*, March 11. http://www.nintendoworldreport.com/ feature/13085/eiji-aonumas-gdc-2007-presentation

Kasson, John F. 1978. *Amusing the Million: Coney Island at the Turn of the Century*. New York: Hill and Wang.

Katsuya, Eguchi, Shigeru Miyamoto, and Takashi Tezuka. Method and Apparatus for Multi-User Communications Using Discrete Video Game Platforms. US Patent 6951516 B1, filed on August 13, 2002, and issued on October 4, 2005.

Kent, Steven L. 2001. *The Ultimate History of Video Games: The Story behind the Craze That Touched Our Lives and Changed the World*. New York: Three Rivers.

"King Kong Toppled." 1984. *Play Meter*, December 15, 19.

Kirby's Adventure. Nintendo. 1993. Video Game.

Kohler, Chris. 2004. *Power Up: How Japanese Video Games Gave the World an Extra Life*. Indianapolis, IN: BrandyGames.

Kohler, Chris. 2008. "Miyamoto Struggles to Sell Inscrutable *Wii Music* Game." *Wired*, October 31. http://www.wired.com/2008/10/miyamoto-wii-mu/

"Like Nothing Anyone's Done Before." n.d. *Iwata Asks: Wii Fit*. http://iwataasks.nintendo.com/interviews/#/wii/wii_fit/0/1

Link's Crossbow Training. 2007. Nintendo. Video Game.

Loguidice, Bill and Matt Barton. 2009. *Vintage Games: An Insider Look at the History of* Grand Theft Auto, Super Mario, *and the Most Influential Games of All Time*. Burlington, MA: Focal Press.

Madden, Orla. 2013. "Miyamoto Discusses Retirement in Recent Interview." *NintendoLife*, March 6. Accessed August 10, 2013.

"Mail Bag." 1988. *Nintendo Fan Club News*, April/May, 2.5: 26.

Mario & Luigi: Partners in Time. 2005. Nintendo. Video Game.

Mario Artist: Paint Studio. 1999. Nintendo. Video Game.

Mario Artist: Talent Studio. 2000. Nintendo. Video Game.

"Mario Couldn't Jump at First." n.d. *Iwata Asks: Super Mario Bros. Wii*. Accessed July 1, 2014. http://iwataasks.nintendo.com/interviews/#/wii/nsmb/0/0

Mario Kart 64. 1996. Nintendo. Video Game.

Mario Paint. 1992. Nintendo. Video Game.

"Mario Paint." 1993. *Nintendo Magazine System*, December Issue 3, 68–71.

"May 13, 2000, Nintendo Power Source." 2000. Interview transcript archived by *Miyamoto Shrine*, via the Internet Archive. https://web.archive.org/web/20110901094310/ http://www.miyamotoshrine.com/theman/interviews/051300.shtml

McAllister, Ken S. 2004. *Game Work: Language, Power, and Computer Game Culture*. Tuscaloosa, AL: University of Alabama Press.

Melissinos, Chris and Patrick O'Rourke. 2013. *The Art of Video Games: From Pac-Man to Mass Effect*. New York: Welcome Books.

Merrick, Jim. 2000. "The Big Gamecube Interview: Part 1." *IGN*. http://www.ign.com/articles/2000/10/20/the-big-gamecube-interview-part-1

Metal Gear Solid: Twin Snakes. 2004. Konami. Video Game.

Metroid. Nintendo. 1996. Video Game.

Mielke, James. 1998. "The Miyamoto Tapes." GameSpot. November 11. http://www.gamespot.com/articles/the-miyamoto-tapes/1100-2465458/

Miyamoto, Shigeru. 1999. "Conference Keynote: Shigeru Miyamoto," keynote speech, GDC 1999. http://www.gdcvault.com/play/1014846/Conference-Keynote-Shigeru

Miyamoto, Shigeru. 2007. "A Creative Vision," keynote speech, Game Developers Conference (GDC), March 8, 2007. Video, http://www.visualwebcaster.com/Nintendo/38232/event.html

Miyamoto, Shigeru. 2011. "On the 25th Anniversary of *The Legend of Zelda*." In *The Legend of Zelda: Hyrule Historia*, edited by Patrick Thorpe, 2–3. Milwaukie, OR: Dark Horse.

Miyamoto, Shigeru, Takao Shimizu, Satoshi Nishiumi, and Kazuo Koshima. Game System Operable with Backup Data on Different Kinds of Game Machines. US Patent 6132315 A, filed on November 12, 1998, and issued on October 17, 2000.

Miyamoto, Shigeru, Yasunari Nashida, Takumi Kawagoe, and Satoshi Nishiumi. Video Game System and Method with Enhanced Three-Dimensional Character and Background Control. US Patent 6155926A, filed May 16, 1997, and issued December 5, 2000.

"Miyamoto: The Interview." 2007. *Edge*, November 27. Accessed August 10, 2013. http://www.computerandvideogames.com/176422/interviews/miyamoto-the-interview/

MotoRace USA. 1982. Irem. Video Game.

"Mr. Miyamoto on Star Fox." 1997. In *Star Fox 64 Official Nintendo Player's Guide*, 116–19. Redmond, WA: Nintendo of America Inc.

Ms. Pac-Man. 1982. Bally Midway / Namco. Video Game.

Munroe, Randall. 2007. "Fucking Blue Shells." *XKCD*, July 16. Comic. https://xkcd.com/290/

Myers, Andy. 2005. "Man's Best Friend: With Nintendogs Set to Make Its Mark on North America, We've Documented the First 11 Days in the Life of a DS Dog." *Nintendo Power* 195: 42–45.

Nintendo. 1985. *Super Mario Bros*. Game Booklet included with *Super Mario Bros*. Distributed by Nintendo.

Nintendo Land. 2012. Nintendo. Video Game.

Nintendo Magazine System. 1993. *Nintendo Magazine System*, December #3.

Nintendo Power. 1987. *Nintendo Power*, vol. 13.

Nintendo Power Strategy Guide: Super Mario Bros. 3. 1990. Redmond, WA: Nintendo of America Inc.

"Nintendo Roundtable." 2002. *IGN*, February 28. http://www.ign.com/
articles/2002/02/28/nintendo-roundtable

Nintendogs. 2005. Nintendo. Video Game.

Nitz, J. C., S. Kyus, R. Isles, and S. Fu. 2010. "Is the Wii Fit a new-generation
tool for improving balance, health, and well-being? A pilot study."
Climacteric 13.5: 487–91.

Nutt, Christian. 2014. "Nintendo discusses plans for smartphones, helping the
Wii U rebound." *Gamasutra*, January 29. http://www.gamasutra.com/view/
news/209625/Nintendo_discusses_plans_for_smartphones_helping_the_
Wii_U_rebound.php

Nutt, Diane and Diane Railton. 2003. "The Sims: Real Life as Genre."
Information, Communication & Society 6.4: 577–92.

"One day, the Louvre." n.d. *Iwata Asks: Nintendo 3DS Guides: Louvre.*
http://iwataasks.nintendo.com/interviews/#/3ds/louvre-guide/0/0

Ono, Sokyo and William P. Woodard. 1962. *Shinto: The Kami Way*. Rutland,
VT: Charles E. Tuttle Co.

Owens, S. G., J. C. Garner 3rd, J. M. Loftin, N. van Blerk, and K. Ermin. 2011.
"Changes in Physical Activity and Fitness After 3 Months of Home Wii
Fit™ Use." *Journal of Strength Conditioning Research* 25.11: 3191–97.

Pac-Man. 1980. Namco. Video Game.

Padala, Kalpana P., Prasad R. Padala, Timothy R. Malloy, Jenenne A. Geske,
Patricia M. Dubbert, Richard A. Dennis, Kimberly K. Garner, Melinda
M. Bopp, William J. Burke, and Dennis H. Sullivan. 2012. "Wii Fit for
Improving Gait and Balance in an Assisted Living Facility: A Pilot Study."
Journal of Aging Research, volume 2012.

Palmer, Greg. 2004. *The Video Game Revolution*, DVD. Seattle, WA: KCTS
Television.

Paper Mario: The Thousand-Year Door. 2004. Nintendo. Video Game.

Parkin, Simon. 2012. "Is Shigeru Miyamoto's Game Over at Nintendo?"
TheGuardian.com Games Blog. http://www.theguardian.com/technology/
gamesblog/2012/apr/26/shigeru-miyamotos-game-over-nintendo

Paumgarten, Nick. 2010. "Master of Play: The Many Worlds of a Video
Game Artist." *The New Yorker*, December 20. http://www.newyorker.com/
magazine/2010/12/20/master-of-play

Pelland, Scott. 2005. "The Kart Connection: Mario Kart DS and the New
Nintendo Wi-Fi Connection Are Set to Fulfill the Promise of the Dual-
Screened Wonder and Lead the Way to a Revolution in Gaming." *Nintendo
Power*, August 2005, 36–39.

Pettus, S. 2012. *Service Games: The Rise and Fall of Sega*. CreateSpace, Independent Publishing Platform.

Pikmin. 2001. Nintendo. Video Game.

Pitfall. 1982. Atari. Video Game.

Plow, Matthew and Marcia Finlayson. 2011. "Potential Benefits of Nintendo Wii Fit Among People with Multiple Sclerosis: A Longitudinal Pilot Study." *International Journal of MS Care* 13.1: 21–30.

Pokémon: Red and Green (JP) or *Pokémon: Red and Blue* (US). 1996. Nintendo. Video Game.

Pole Position. 1982. Namco / Atari. Video Game.

PONG. 1972. Atari. Video Game.

"Pro's Corner." 1987. *Nintendo Fan Club News*, Winter 1987, 1.4: 20.

Radar Scope. 1979. Nintendo. Video Game.

Reisinger, Don. 2007. "Don't believe the hype: Super Mario Galaxy is not that great." *CNet*, November 26. http://www.cnet.com/news/dont-believe-the-hype-super-mario-galaxy-is-not-that-great/

RoadBlasters. 1987. Atari. Video Game.

Robinson, Phil Aledn. 2001. *Band of Brothers*, Television show. New York: HBO.

Rock Band. 2007. Harmonix / Pi Studios. Video Game.

Roller Coaster Tychoon. 1999. Hasbro Interactive. Video Game.

Ruggill, Judd Ethan and Ken S. McAllister. 2011. *Gaming Matters: Art, Science Magic, and the Computer Game Medium*. Tuscaloosa, AL: University of Alabama Press.

Ryan, Jeff. 2011. *Super Mario: How Nintendo Conquered America*. New York: Portfolio / Penguin.

Salen, Katie and Eric Zimmerman. 2004. *Rules of Play: Game Design Fundamentals*. Cambridge, MA: The MIT Press.

Sayre, Carolyn. 2007. "10 Questions for Shigeru Miyamoto." *Time Magazine*, July 19. Accessed August 2, 2014. http://content.time.com/time/magazine/article/0,9171,1645158,00.html

Schilling, Chris. 2011. "Shigeru Miyamoto: 'I'm the Person who saw Things Differently.'" *The Guardian*, April 30. http://www.theguardian.com/technology/2011/may/01/shigeru-miyamoto-nintendo-donkey-kong

Sheff, David. 1994. *Game Over: How Nintendo Conquered the World*. New York: Random House.

Shenkar, Oded. 2010. "Copycats: How Smart Companies use Imitation to Gain a Strategic Edge." *Strategic Direction* 26.10: 3–5.

Sheriff. Version 1: Japanese. Exidy. Nintendo. 1979. Video Game.

"Shigeru Miyamoto's Early Encounters with Music." n.d. *Iwata Asks: Super Mario Bros. Wii.* Accessed July 1, 2014. http://iwataasks.nintendo.com/ interviews/#/wii/wii_music/0/0

"Shigeru Miyamoto Roundtable." 2001. *IGN,* June 11. http://www.ign.com/ articles/2001/06/11/shigeru-miyamoto-roundtable-part-i

"Shigeru Miyamoto Talk Asia Interview." 2007. CNN.com. http://www.cnn. com/2007/WORLD/asiapcf/02/14/miyamoto.script/

Silverman, Barry G., Michael Johns, Ransom Weaver, and Joshua Mosley. 2003. "Authoring Edutainment Stories for Online Players (AESOP): Introducing Gameplay into Interactive Dramas." *Virtual Storytelling: Using Virtual Reality Technologies for Storytelling* 2897: 65–73.

Sinfield, George. 2006. "The Wii Experience." *Nintendo Power,* July 2006, vol. 205, 33–37.

Sinfield, George. 2007. "Living the Hy Life." *Nintendo Power,* January 2007, vol. 211, 48–54.

Smith, Robert P. and Steven D. Eppinger. 1997. "A Predictive Model of Sequential Iteration in Engineering Design." *Management Science* 43.8: 1104–20.

Snyder, Nick. 2012. "The Legend of Miyamoto: How Nintendo Shaped UX." *UX Magazine.* http://uxmag.com/articles/the-legend-of-miyamoto-how-nintendo-shaped-ux

Sonic the Hedgehog. Sonic Team. 1991. Video Game.

Space Invaders. 1978. Taito Corporation. Video Game.

Speed Race. 1974. Taito. Video Game.

Speilberg, Steven. 1998. *Saving Private Ryan.* Universal City, CA: DreamWorks Pictures.

Star Fox. 1993. Nintendo. Video Game.

Star Fox 64. 1997. Nintendo. Video Game.

Super Mario 64. 1996. Nintendo. Video Game.

Super Mario Bros. 1985. Nintendo. Video Game.

Super Mario Bros. Booklet. 1985. Nintendo. Packaged with Video Game.

Super Mario Bros. 3. 1988. Nintendo. Video Game.

Super Mario Galaxy. 2007. Nintendo. Video Game.

Super Mario Galaxy 2. 2010. Nintendo. Video Game.

Super Mario Kart. 1992. Nintendo. Video Game.

"Super Mario Kart." 1993. *Nintendo Magazine System,* December Issue 3, 40–45.

Super Mario RPG. 1996. Nintendo. Video Game.

"Super Play Magazine Interviews Shigeru Miyamoto about *The Legend of Zelda*." 2003. Reproduced on *Nintendo Forums*, November 14, 2009. Accessed August 2, 2014. www.nintendoforums.com/articles/40/super-play-magazine-interviews-shigeru-miyamoto-about-zelda

Super Smash Bros. 1999. Nintendo. Video Game.

Sutton-Smith, Brian. 1997. *The Ambiguity of Play.* Cambridge, MA: Harvard University Press.

Taiko no Tatsujin. 2001. Namco. Video Game.

Tamagotchi. 1996. Bandai. Video Game.

Taylor, Jes. 2014. "E3 2014 Rumors: Nintendo and Its Rumors To Save Wii U." *B-TEN*, May 30. http://b-ten.com/e3-rumors-nintendo/

"The Game Guys." 1996. *Nintendo Power*, January, vol. 80, 24–25.

"The Importance of Being Aware of One's Body." n.d. *Iwata Asks: Wii Fit.* http://iwataasks.nintendo.com/interviews/#/wii/wii_fit/0/4

"The Indefinable Essence of Zelda." n.d. *Iwata Asks: The Legend of Zelda: Twilight Princess.* http://iwataasks.nintendo.com/interviews/#/wii/twilight_princess/0/0

"The Joy of Playing Music." n.d. *Iwata Asks: Wii Music.* Accessed August 1, 2014. http://iwataasks.nintendo.com/interviews/#/wii/wii_music/0/2

"The Legend of Miyamoto." 1998. *Nintendo Power*, August, 52–57.

The Legend of Zelda. 1986. Nintendo. Video Game.

The Legend of Zelda Booklet. 1986. Game Booklet included with *The Legend of Zelda.* Video Game. Nintendo.

The Legend of Zelda: Ocarina of Time. 1998. Nintendo. Video Game.

The Legend of Zelda: The Wind Waker. 2002. Nintendo. Video Game.

The Legend of Zelda: Twilight Princess. 2006. Nintendo. Video Game.

"The Man Behind Mario." 1991. *Mario Mania Player's Guide.* Nintendo of America, 30–32.

"The 'Process' as the Reward." n.d. *Iwata Asks: Link's Crossbow Training.* Accessed July 1, 2014. https://www.nintendo.co.za/Iwata-Asks/Iwata-Asks-Link-s-Crossbow-Training/Iwata-Asks-Link-s-Crossbow-Training/2-The-process-as-the-reward/2-The-process-as-the-reward-206090.html

The Sims. 2000. Electronic Arts. Video Game.

Timothy, Christopher, John Stamper, Timothy David Joseph Stamper, Mark Alexis Edmonds, Russell William Irwin, Beau Ner Chesluk, Hirokazu Tanaka, Takashi Ohno, Noriaki Teramoto, Shigeru Miyamoto,

Takao Shimizu, Satoshi Nishiumi, and Kazuo Koshima. System and Method for Automatically Editing Capturing Images for Inclusion into 3D Video Game Play. US Patent 6894686 B2, filed on May 15, 2001, and issued on May 17, 2005.

Tobin, Joseph J., ed. 1992. *Re-Made in Japan: Everyday Life and Consumer Taste in a Changing Society*. New Haven, CT: Yale University Press.

Tobin, Samuel. 2013. *Portable Play in Everyday Life: The Nintendo DS*. New York: Palgrave Macmillan.

Totu, Florian. 2009. "Nowadays, Shigeru Miyamoto Would Not Be Hired By Nintendo." *Softpedia*, November 24. Accessed August 9, 2013. http://news.softpedia.com/news/Nowadays-Shigeru-Miyamoto-Would-Not-Be-Hired-by-Nintendo-127816.shtml

Tovey, Michael. 1997. "Styling and Design: Intuition and Analysis in Industrial Design." *Design Studies* 18.1: 5–31.

Trottier, David. 2014. *The Screenwriter's Bible: A Complete Guide to Writing, Formatting, and Selling Your Script*. Los Angeles, CA: Silman-James Press.

Tuan, Yi-Fu. 1977. *Space and place: The Perspective of Experience*. Minneapolis: University of Minnesota Press.

"Using the D-pad to Jump." n.d. *Iwata Asks: Wii*. http://iwataasks.nintendo.com/interviews/#/wii/mario25th/4/0

Vernadakis, Nikolaos, Asimenia Gioftsidou, Panagoitis Antoniou, Dionysis Ioannidis, and Maria Giannousi. 2012. "The impact of Nintendo Wii to physical education students' balance compared to the traditional approaches." *Computers and Education* 59.2: 196–205.

VG Chartz. 2014. "Mario Paint." *VGChartz, Games DB*. Accessed August 1, 2014. http://www.vgchartz.com/game/3716/mario-paint/

VG Chartz. 2014. "Platform Totals." *VGChartz*. Accessed August 28, 2014. http://www.vgchartz.com/analysis/platform_totals/

VG Chartz. 2014. "Super Mario 64." *VGChartz, Games DB*. Accessed August 1, 2014. http://www.vgchartz.com/game/2278/super-mario-64/

VG Chartz. 2014. "Super Mario Galaxy." *VGChartz, Games DB*. Accessed August 9, 2014. http://www.vgchartz.com/game/6963/super-mario-galaxy/

VG Chartz. 2014. "Super Nintendo Entertainment System." *VGChartz, Console StatistiGames DB*. Accessed August 9, 2014. http://www.vgchartz.com/platform/11/super-nintendo-entertainment-system/

VG Chartz. 2014. "Tamagotchi." *VGChartz, Games DB*. Accessed August 9, 2014. http://www.vgchartz.com/game/3333/tamagotchi/

VG Chartz. 2014. "The Legend of Zelda: The Wind Waker." *VGChartz, Games DB*. Accessed August 20, 2014. http://www.vgchartz.com/game/2400/the-legend-of-zelda-the-wind-waker/

VG Chartz. 2014. "Wii Fit." *VGChartz, Games DB*. Accessed August 9, 2014. http://www.vgchartz.com/game/7480/wii-fit/

VG Chartz. 2014. "Wii Music." *VGChartz, Games DB*. Accessed August 9, 2014. http://www.vgchartz.com/game/24657/wii-music/

"Virgin Megastore Eiki Aonuma and Shigeru Miyamoto—February 21st 2003." 2003. Interview transcript archived by *Zeldadungeon.net*. http://www.zeldadungeon.net/Interviews-2003-02-21-Virgin-Megastore-Eiji-Aonuma-Shigeru-Miyamoto.php

Welsh, Oli. 2014. "Iwata isn't Nintendo's problem. It's Miyamoto." *Eurogamer.net*, January 25. http://www.eurogamer.net/articles/2014-01-25-iwata-isnt-nintendos-problem-its-miyamoto

Wendel, Johnathan. 2007. "The 2007 TIME 100: Shigeru Miyamoto." *TIME Magazine*, May 3. http://content.time.com/time/specials/2007/time100/article/0,28804,1595326_1615737_1615521,00.html

Wesley, David and Gloria Barczak. 2010. *Innovation and Marketing in the Video Game Industry: Avoiding the Performance Trap*. Surrey, UK: Gower / Ashgate Publishing.

Whitehead, Thomas. 2012. "Feature: Shigeru Miyamoto—The Father of Modern Video Games." *Nintendo Life*, November 16. http://www.nintendolife.com/news/2012/11/feature_shigeru_miyamoto_the_father_of_modern_video_games

Wii Fit. 2007. Nintendo. Video Game.

Wii Music. 2008. Nintendo. Video Game.

Wii Sports. 2005. Nintendo. Video Game.

Wolf, Mark J. P. and Bernard Perron. 2010. *The Video Game Theory Reader*. New York: Routledge.

World Golf Tour. 2008. Nelson and Chang. Video Game.

World of Warcraft. 2004. Blizzard. Video Game.

Yanagisawa, Tetsuya. 2007. *Aoi Sekai no Chuushin de*. Television show, Red Road.

"Yukio Kaneoka." VGMdb. Last edited May 10, 2011. Accessed August 10, 2014. http://vgmdb.net/artist/1342

Index